RELIGION IN LIFE CURRICULUM

Edited by Edward A. Fitzpatrick, Ph.D.

SECOND GRADE TEACHERS PLAN BOOK AND MANUAL

HIGHWAY TO HEAVEN SERIES

BOOK OF THE HOLY CHILD (Grade One)

LIFE OF MY SAVIOR (Grade Two)

LIFE OF THE SOUL (Grade Three)

BEFORE CHRIST CAME (Grade Four)

THE VINE AND THE BRANCHES (Grade Five)

THE MISSAL (Grade Six)

HIGHWAY TO GOD (Grades Seven and Eight)

Accompanying this Series is the RELIGION IN LIFE CURRICULUM for grades one to six and PRACTICAL PROBLEMS IN RELIGION for grades seven and eight.

Religion in Life Curriculum

Second Grade Teachers Plan Book and Manual

Designed for use with the
HIGHWAY TO HEAVEN SERIES
of Catechism Textbooks

ST. AUGUSTINE ACADEMY PRESS
HOMER GLEN, ILLINOIS

Nihil obstat:
     H. B. RIES,
          Censor librorum

Imprimatur:
     ✠ SAMUEL A. STRITCH,
          Archiepiscopus Milwaukiensis

October 25, 1933

This book was originally published in 1933 by The Bruce Publishing Company.
This edition reprinted in 2018 by St. Augustine Academy Press.
ISBN: 978-1-64051-024-1

EDITOR'S NOTE TO THE REPRINTED EDITION:

In reassembling this *Religion in Life Curriculum*, we thought it best to include excerpts from the curriculum overview volume, titled *Curriculum in Religion*, which was published in 1931 as the basis for development of the fleshed-out Teachers Plan Book and Manual before you. In that original volume, the entire curriculum for first through eighth grades were laid out in basic outline form, with attention given to the main focus, goals and resources for each grade. You may find that some of the resources listed in these excerpts did not find their way into the current manual. However, we felt it would be helpful to the teacher (or parent) to see a summary of the intended vision for the current year.

In the appendix found at the rear of this volume, we have also provided a comprehensive listing of all the recommended resources found in this manual, to which we have added notations showing the most frequently used and/or most helpful resources, as well as those which can be found online.

Lastly, please note that most of the recommended student readings (that is, those which would have been found in the various school readers listed throughout this book) have been assembled and printed under one cover in the new *Magnificat Readers* which accompany this series.

Lisa Bergman

St. Augustine Academy Press
February 2018

CONTENTS

CONTENTS

The following section is an excerpt from the book "A Curriculum in Religion," included for the convenience of teachers as a way of familiarizing themselves with the basic goals laid out for the Religion in Life Curriculum for the Second Grade.

RELIGION IN GRADE II

Main Interest: The Public Life of Christ

THE main subject matter of the second grade is the public life of Christ. Reviewing the first thirty years of the life of Christ at the beginning of the year, the child then takes up in detail the public life from the baptism by John to the Ascension.

Outline of Main Topics

The topics to be studied include a simple presentation of the following events:

A. *Public Life to the Passion*
  1. John the Baptist and the Christ
  2. The Temptation of Christ
  3. The First Miracle of Cana
  4. Other Miracles
  5. The Twelve Apostles are Chosen
  6. The Sermon on the Mount
  7. Some Parables
  8. The Multiplication of the Loaves
  9. Second Multiplication of Loaves
  10. The Transfiguration
  11. Training the Apostles
  12. Seventy-Two Disciples
  13. Mary and Martha
  14. More Parables

This completes the *introduction* to the religious education by a fairly detailed presentation of the life of Christ within the comprehension of the child. The emphasis is not on doctrine but on love for the Master. The further development will be to have his "love abound more and more in knowledge."

Quotations

The quotations listed should be learned at the time the facts of Christ's public life are being studied, which gives them significance. The quotations in this grade emphasize the Divinity of Christ, the Son of God. The briefer ones at least should be learned as a result of the repetition of it in the instructions. The list for grade three follows:

"The Father loveth the Son: and He hath given all things into His hand" (John iii. 35).

"I am the Good Shepherd, and I know Mine, and Mine know Me" (John x. 14).

"This is My beloved Son, in Whom I am well pleased" (Matt. iii. 16–17; xvii. 5).

"Jesus saith to them: But Whom do you say that I am? Simon Peter answered and said: Thou art Christ, the Son of the living God" (Matt. xvi. 15–16).

"Jesus saith to him: Thou hast said *it*. Nevertheless I say to you, hereafter you shall see the Son of Man sitting on the right hand of the power of God, and coming in the clouds of heaven.

"Then the high priest rent his garments, saying: He hath blasphemed; what further need have we of witnesses? Behold, now you have heard the blasphemy" (Matt. xxvi. 64–65).

"And I saw, and I gave testimony, that this is the Son of God" (John i. 34).

"For God so loved the world, as to give His only begotten Son; that whosoever believeth in Him, may not perish, but may have life everlasting" (John iii. 16).

"And they that were in the boat came and adored Him, saying: Indeed Thou art the Son of God" (Matt. xiv. 33).

"Nathaniel answered Him, and said: Rabbi, Thou art the Son of God, Thou art the King of Israel" (John i. 49).

"She saith to Him: Yea, Lord, I have believed that Thou art Christ the Son of the living God, Who art come into this world" (John xi. 27).

"The Jews answered Him: We have a law; and according to the law He ought to die, because He made Himself the Son of God" (John xix. 7).

"And Pilate wrote a title also, and he put it upon the cross. And the writing was: JESUS OF NAZARETH, THE KING OF THE JEWS" (John xix. 19).

"And the centurion who stood over against Him, seeing that crying out in this manner He had given up the ghost, said: Indeed this Man was the Son of God" (Mark xv. 39).

"And then shall appear the sign of the Son of Man in heaven: and then shall all tribes of the earth mourn: and they shall see the Son of Man coming in the clouds of heaven with much power and majesty" (Matt. xxiv. 30).

"My Lord and my God" (John xx. 28).

"Blessed are the poor in spirit: for theirs is the kingdom of heaven.

"Blessed are the meek: for they shall possess the land.

"Blessed are they that mourn: for they shall be comforted.

"Blessed are they that hunger and thirst after justice: for they shall have their fill.

"Blessed are the merciful: for they shall obtain mercy.

"Blessed are the clean of heart: for they shall see God.

"Blessed are the peacemakers: for they shall be called the children of God.

"Blessed are they that suffer persecution for justice' sake: for theirs is the kingdom of heaven.

"Blessed are ye when they shall revile you, and persecute you, and speak all that is evil against you, untruly, for My sake" (Matt. v. 3–11).

Activities

For supplementary activities the parables offer opportunities for dramatizations.

The Ten Virgins (Matt. xxv. 1–13).

The Good Samaritan (Luke x. 30–37).

The Marriage of the King's Son (Matt. xxii. 1–14).

The parables offer, too, an opportunity for an elaboration of the parables as an approach to creative writing. This is especially true of the parables relating to the kingdom of heaven and its Head.

Booklets begun in previous grades might be continued, or new booklets might be begun on:

The Passion of Christ (using the "Stations of the Cross"),

The Parables of Christ,

The Miracles of Christ,

The Apostles of Christ,

The Appearances of Christ after the Resurrection.

A doctrinal booklet might be made stating the principal doctrinal points under the heading: "*I believe.*"

The public life of Christ offers opportunity for illustration.

Pictures

The children should know the following pictures, which should be presented in connection with the stories studied. Some should be made a matter of special study:

John the Baptist Preaching in the Wilderness — *Doré*
St. John in the Desert — *Raphael*
Temptation of Jesus — *Cornicelius*
The Temptation — *Hoffmann*
The Miracle of Cana — *Tintoretto*
Marriage at Cana — *Doré*
Christ and the Money Changers — *Hoffmann*
Miraculous Draught of Fishes — *Doré*
Christ, the Consoler — *Plockhurst*
Christ Healing the Sick — *Schonherr*
Sermon on the Mount — *Hoffmann*
Sermon on the Mount — *Bida*
Jesus Preaching to the Multitude — *Doré*
Jesus Stilling the Tempest — *Doré*
Jesus Blessing Little Children — *Plockhurst*
Christ Blessing Little Children — *Hoffmann*
Christ Healing the Blind Man — *Bida*
Christ Healing the Ten Lepers — *Seifert*
Christ Healing the Sick — *Hoffmann*
Christ Raising Jairus' Daughter — *Richter*
Raising the Dead — *Hoffmann*
The Daughter of Jairus — *Hoffmann*
Christ and Widow of Naim — *Verchio*
Christ and the Rich Young Man — *Hoffmann*
The Good Samaritan — *Anonymous*
Divine Shepherd — *Murillo*
Prodigal Son — *Molitor*

Good Shepherd — *Dobson*
The Last Supper — *Zimmerman*
Last Supper — *Gebhardt*
Last Supper — *Da Vinci*
Kiss of Judas — *Geiger*
Christ in Gethsemane — *Hoffmann*
Christ in Gethsemane — *Liska*
Easter — *Thomson*
He is Risen — *Plockhurst*
Easter Morning — *Plockhurst*
To Emmaus — *Hoffmann*
On the Way to Emmaus — *Plockhurst*

Religious Vocabulary

Special care must be taken to see that the child's religious vocabulary is increased in connection particularly with the main topic of the grade, and that the new words are taught as the need develops and in the actual situation. Care should be taken to review words previously learned and to be sure a correct meaning is given to them on the child's own level. The words should grow in connotation as his religious knowledge and experience increases.

Words that will generally be taught in this grade are:

Zachary	kingdom	testament
Gabriel	scribes	priests
synagogue	transfiguration	Pilate
miracle	Cæsar	Barabbas
sermon	prodigal son	thorns
disciple	Peter	crucify
centurion	Zebedee	Golgotha
Pharisees	David	forsaken
Samaritans	money-changers	Mary Magdalene
Satan	commandments	sepulcher
David	Jerusalem	resurrection

parable	marriage	Judea
everlasting	betrayed	Galilee
kiss	Judas	scourged

Each teacher will be required to make up her specific lists for her specific children. No stress need be placed on the spelling of these words at present. They may be left on the board for reference.

Poems

The following poems carry on somewhat the same themes as the second grade, and furnish an excellent opportunity for reviewing the whole list. There should be reviewed especially those poems relating to the public life of Christ. The suggestive list follows:

How Children Should Live, Isaac Watts
A Child's Evening Prayer, Samuel Taylor Coleridge
My Neighbor, Father Tabb
A Child's Thought at Christmas, Mary Jane Carr
The Mother of Christ, Aubrey De Vere
The Helper, Rev. Hugh Francis Blunt
The Lowest Place, Christina G. Rossetti
What Have I, Christina G. Rossetti
The Blessed Virgin Mary, H. W. Longfellow
Speak, Little Voice, Rev. Michael Earls, S.J.
Four Things, Henry Van Dyke
A Useful Lesson, Rev. M. Russell, S.J.
For Right is Right, Since God is God, Father Faber
Our Hearts were Made for Thee, O Lord, St. Augustine
Hours are Golden Links, God's Token, Adelaide A. Procter
A Song, Charles L. O'Donnell, C.S.C.
Different Ways, Mary Dixon Thayer
Blessed Candle, Joseph Kinney Collins
A Prayer to Mary, Father H. G. Hughes
Thoughts, Mary Dixon Thayer
The Very Time, Mary Dixon Thayer

Poplars, Joseph Kinney Collins
Trees, Joyce Kilmer
Sheep and Lambs, Katherine Tynan
Flower and Weed, Elvira S. Miller
Communion, Caroline Giltinan
Like One I Know, Nancy Campbell
The Making of Birds, Katherine Tynan
Nails, Leonard Feeney, S.J.
Holy Innocents, Christina G. Rossetti
The Tempest, James T. Fields
Our Lord and Our Lady, Hilaire Belloc
Come to Jesus, Father Faber
Little Things, Rev. F. W. Faber
After a Visit to the Blessed Sacrament, S. M. St. John
Finding You, Mary Dixon Thayer
Child of Nazareth, Rev. J. B. Tabb
A Child's Wish, Rev. Abram J. Ryan
Thanksgiving, Mary Dixon Thayer
Discontent, Sarah Orne Jewett

Additional poems should be used emphasizing the public life of Christ which is the center of interest in the grade. Children should be encouraged to "learn by heart" as many poems as possible. All should be required to learn some; many of the poems should be left to the student's own taste. The more difficult poems will be read to the class by the teacher; some poems will be read for their general idea without detailed study, and some poems will be studied in detail. Poems dealing with the same subject in earlier grades should be recalled to mind after the first reading of new poems. The poems suggested above, with others, are included in *Religious Poems for Children, Primary Grades,* (Bruce).

Aspirations and Brief Prayers

As opportunity offers, the following aspirations or others will be taught. One might be selected and written on the board each month, calling attention to it as opportunity permits. The students might prepare aspirations of their own.

1. Jesus, my God, I love Thee above all things.
2. My Lord and my God.
3. O sweet Heart of Jesus, I implore, that I may ever love Thee more and more.
4. Lord, have mercy on us (3),
   Christ, have mercy on us (3),
   Lord, have mercy on us (3).
5. Lord, save us, we perish.
6. Jesus, meek and humble of heart, make my heart like unto Thine.
7. Jesus, I adore Thee.
8. Jesus, Mary, and Joseph, I love Thee.
9. Blessed be Jesus Christ, true God and true Man.
10. Blessed be the great Mother of God, Mary most holy.
11. Let us give thanks to the Lord, our God.
12. Lord, Thou knowest that I love Thee.
13. Lord, teach me to pray.

Prayers

As the child develops, the form of prayers he will learn will change. The form of morning prayer will undoubtedly change from the simplest form to the use of the liturgical prayers of the Church. This will be generally the development. There will be, of course, an increase in the number of prayers, so that by the end of the elementary school the student will be acquainted with the principal prayers of the Church.

1. Morning prayers
2. Evening prayers
3. Grace before meals
4. Grace after meals
5. Act of Contrition
6. Act of Faith
7. Act of Hope
8. Act of Charity
9. Stations of the Cross
10. The Gloria

Hymns

Hymns are an important factor in reënforcing the general religious instruction and training, valuable for their own content, and, if properly taught, add an element of joy to religious instruction that is quite important. The child should, at the end of instruction, know the great hymns of the Church. For the third grade there is suggested the following to be sung within the voice range of the children:

1. Jesus, Jesus Come to Me
2. Virgin Dearest Mother Mine
3. Little King so Fair and Sweet
4. The Child's Christmas Hymn
5. The Child at Close of Day
6. Mother, Dear, O Pray for Me
7. When Our Saviour Wished to Prove
8. Immaculate Mother
9. Jesus, Tender Shepherd

10. Oh, Sacrament Blessed
11. Holy God We Praise Thy Name

Liturgy

The children should be able to identify the liturgical vestments of the priest at Mass: amice, alb, cincture, maniple, stole, and chasuble. It would be highly desirable for the child to see the priest actually put on his vestments.

Upon visit of a bishop or archbishop for confirmation or for other reasons, the vestments of the bishop or archbishop should be taught. If such an event should not happen while the children are in this grade, the instruction should be given when it does happen. The appointment of a new bishop or archbishop should be used for this purpose, as well as to teach other facts about the Church.

Useful supplementary material for the study of various aspects of the liturgy will be found in Fr. Dunney's *The Mass* (Macmillan), and Fr. M. S. Mac-Mahon's *Liturgical Catechism* (Gill & Son, Dublin), and in the *St. Andrew's Daily Missal* by Dom Le Febvre, O.S.B. (Lohmann).

Religious Practice

A definite part of the program in every grade is to build up the practice of religion in every grade and have the development cumulative throughout the grades. Wherever teachers see opportunity to build up Catholic practice, they should do so. Teachers must not confound the lessons that may be essential and the actual practice in the life of the child. The pupil should understand the importance of interior disposition.

In the assignment, to grade the purpose is to provide a specific time to see that the practice is established and understood. In some cases the habit will have been established. The cumulative listing of these practices is to emphasize the fact that they are not taught or established once and you are through with them. The practice must continue to be stimulated until it is "securely rooted in the life of the individual."

There should be emphasized in this grade:

1. Morning Prayer
2. Evening Prayer
3. Regular attendance at Mass on Sundays
4. Attendance at Mass on all holydays of obligation
5. Angelus
6. Bowing at the name of Jesus
7. Tipping hat or bowing as one passes church
8. Tipping hat when one meets Priest or Sister or other religious
9. Monthly Communion or more frequently

Practical Life

The translation of the religious knowledge, practice, and attitudes in the day-to-day life of the child must always be an objective in religious education. The elevation of the actual daily life of the individual to a supernatural plane will come about through the character of the individual's motivation. This must be a matter of development; the child must be taken, however, where he is. The lines of development are indicated but the more specific content is left for the experimentation of the first year. A teacher should always take advantage of any actual situation, and should always strive to meet difficulties which her children as a group are confronted with, no matter whether it is included in the course of study or not.

1. Do a good turn every day for the love of God.
   a) Daily examination of conscience at night.
   b) Daily specific review of day's thoughts, words, or deeds.
   c) Weekly complete examination of conscience for confession or as a preparation for spiritual Communion.
   d) Daily expiation for the temporal punishment due to sin.
2. Cultivation of virtuous life.
3. Cultivation of school virtues.
4. Promotion of corporal and spiritual works of mercy.

Special attention is directed to the chapters on "The Christian Rule of Life" and "The Christian Daily Exercise" of the *Catechism of Christian Doctrine* approved by the Cardinal, Archbishops, and Bishops of England and Wales, and directed to be used in all their dioceses.

Christian Doctrine

In this grade, perhaps the main contribution to doctrinal teaching will be the specific content of the articles on the Creed on Jesus Christ, His divinity, the facts of His humanity, the second person of the Blessed Trinity, the Savior and Redeemer of men, and particularly the crucifixion, resurrection, and ascension. Growing out of this will be a fuller statement of the facts of His life leading to the establishment of the sacrament of penance, the promise of the Holy Ghost and the descent of the Holy Ghost on the Apostles; the establishment of the Church and of the new priesthood. The basis for the later discussion of the miracles of Christ and of establishment of the sacraments is laid here.

Basal Text and Supplementary Material

The basal text for this grade will be Sr. Bartholomew's, *The Public Life of Christ*, (Bruce) which gives the material on this level. A valuable supplement will be Berdice Moran's story of the public life in verse, *Verse for Tiny Tots*, (Bruce). These are texts prepared to carry out specifically the content of this course of study. They will be used experimentally the first year as a basis for revision if necessary to meet actual classroom conditions.

Further supplementary material may be found in:

1. The Gospels.

2. Mother Loyola, *Jesus of Nazareth*, (Benziger).

3. Sr. James Stanislaus, *Journeys of Jesus*, (Ginn), Book I, II, III.

4. Mary Eaton, *The Little Ones*, (Herder).

5. Josephine Van Dyke Brownson, *To the Heart of a Child*, (Universal Knowledge Foundation).

6. Rev. A. J. Moss, S.J., *Life of Jesus Christ*.

7. Rev. Hugh Pope, *A Catholic Student's Aids to the Bible*, Vol. 5, (Kenedy), (Revised Ed.), (for texts of same incidents in the different Gospels).

8. Sr. Mary Aurelia and Rev. Felix Kirsch, *Practical Aids for Catholic Teachers*, (Benziger).

RELIGION IN GRADE II

INTRODUCTION

The Course in Religion, Grade II, is a detailed development of the Outlines for a Course in Religion for the Grades, edited by Doctor Edward Fitzpatrick, Dean of the Graduate School, Marquette University.

The text for Grade II in Religion is *The Life of My Savior*.

In the Teacher's Manual each of the lessons in *The Life of My Savior* has been developed according to the following headings:

TO THE TEACHER

INTRODUCTION

PRESENTATION

DEVELOPMENTS

    Doctrine, Prayer, Hymns, Poems, Quotations, Virtuous Practices, Creative Music, Booklets, Dramatizations, Programs, Self-Expression, Creative Art, Picture Studies

PICTURES

PUPIL'S READINGS

    All the stories listed under Pupil's Readings are taken from second-grade readers

TEACHER'S REFERENCES

TEACHER'S NOTES

(The above headings are described in the Introduction under "Suggestions to Teachers.")

Pictures

"You must look at pictures studiously, earnestly, honestly. It will take years before you come to a full appreciation of art; but when at last you have it, you will be possessed of the purest, loftiest, and most ennobling pleasure that the civilized world can offer you."—*John Van Dyke.*

A really good picture is an invaluable asset to every teacher. It at once draws the attention of the child, it gives a clear impression to him, stimulates his desire for imitation, and quickens his imagination. The teacher in Religion should use as many pictures as possible in connection with the daily lesson. For this purpose it would be well to keep in separate files the pictures collected for each unit. The pictures should be Catholic in conception, and, if possible, attractively colored. The children also could be interested in making their collection or in adding to the school collection of pictures.

Picture Studies, by Theodore M. Dillaway, in loose-leaf form, at two cents each, are available at the Picture and Art Craft Shop, 622 Beaumont Street, Saint Paul, Minnesota. This company also offers in one-cent sizes, $3\frac{1}{2}$ by $4\frac{1}{2}$, beautifully colored prints of famous art pictures.

A wall picture has been suggested in various lessons of this Course. The following are appropriate for Grade II and are beautifully colored:

Title	Size	Price
The Sacred Heart of Jesus—Zabateri	28 by 39	$2.50
The Sacred Heart of Mary—Zabateri	28 by 39	2.50
The Guardian Angel—Feuerstein	25 by 36	2.00
St. Joseph—Enrico Reffo	23 by 35	2.00
The Good Shepherd—Untersberger	18 by 37	4.50
Jesus with Mary and Martha—Untersberger	20 by 30	4.50
Healing the Sick—Max	22 by 28	2.00
Christ Blessing Children—Schmidt	22 by 28	2.00
Christ's Entry into Jerusalem—Plockhorst	22 by 28	2.00
The Last Supper—Da Vinci	22 by 28	2.00

All the above pictures in beautiful tints are available at Diedrich-Schaefer Co., Milwaukee, Wisconsin.

Other Material

Paper Statuettes, Christ in the Crib, 100 for $1.75

The Way of the Cross, Post Card, No. 1932, Geb. Fugel, in original colors; 3 sets, 60 cents

The Seven Last Words, No. 3294, Geb. Fugel, in original colors; set, 25 cents

New Papier-Maché Crib Set, twelve figures:

Figures 2½ inches, 75 cents a set

Figures 4½ inches, $2.00 a set

All the above material is available at Diedrich-Schaefer Co.*

Points for Picture Study in Grade II

Short, interesting sketch of the painter's life.

What the painter is particularly noted for in his pictures; e.g., Correggio, *light* and *music*.

The setting of the picture in the artist's life.

Artistic points about the picture which the teacher will bring out by good questions. Most important is to let the children tell what they like in the picture; why they like it; what story the picture tells them.

The children may dramatize the pictures. It is of great interest and value for children to reproduce the various poses and actions in the picture. At times children may be arranged into groups, each group to represent one picture, while the other groups tell the story which the living picture represents. Simple costuming will add much to the effectiveness of this plan.

Appropriate music, songs, suggestive of the picture, may be sung while studying the picture or dramatizing it. With the study of Holy Night, the hymn "Holy Night, Silent Night" should be sung.

The children should be encouraged to make their own picture book of the pictures studied during the Religion Hour.

---

*Rubber stamps of religious themes, e.g., Jesus in the Crib, Angels, with which to work out any of the stories in pictures and then to color these, may be had from the Creative Educational Society, Mankato, Minnesota.

INTRODUCTION TO THE LESSON

The Introduction to each lesson is merely a suggestion as to how the day's story might be approached. An effort has been made in the course to link up each lesson as closely as possible to that preceding, so that the child will have not only specific knowledge of the doctrine, but a general notion as to the meaning of the Unit and of the year's work as well.

The Introductions have been varied, including the following suggestions: review questions, songs, poems, dramatizations, stories, oral and silent reading, socialized discussions.

Presentation

The teacher will frequently tell the story in its entirety. She will have the children grouped about her informally and tell them the story in an attractive and deeply religious manner. She will speak to them and permit them to ask a question about the story at any time.

The wording of the stories as given in the Presentations is merely suggestive. It is understood that the teacher does not use the story verbatim, but rather that she adapt her language as far as possible to the comprehension of the children. When necessary she will explain the meaning of new or unusual words, according to any authorized method of learning new words and phrases.

At times the children should be grouped into smaller divisions and, with one elected as their chairman, should conduct their own class, telling the story to each other and asking each other questions about it.

They should be encouraged frequently to tell the beautiful story to mother and father, or to read it to them and to the family at home, and to their friends.

Doctrine or "I Believe" Booklet

Since the underlying thought to be kept before the minds of the children the entire second year is: *Jesus Is God and Man, I Must Live and Die for Him*, a booklet on doctrine would be very appropriate. Let this booklet run parallel with the work of the entire year. On the average, take one truth a week as it naturally occurs in the week's lessons; e.g., in the lesson on the Trinity, let the children draw in their booklet a shamrock on the leaves of which they will write the words: *Father, Son, Holy Ghost*. Under their drawing they write the sentence: I believe in the Holy Trinity, One God in Three Persons. In the lesson on Creation they could write: I believe that God made all things. I believe that God made me. I believe heaven is my true Home, or any similar expressions of belief.

Whenever possible, the children should illustrate the "I Believe" sentence with pictures or original drawings.

Let the children suggest which sentences the class should write in their booklet for the week. The various sentences can be written on the board and the children may select the sentence which they wish. In this way the teacher will know that no error in doctrine has been written. At times the teacher herself will suggest the doctrine sentence she feels is of greatest importance.

Doctrine

In the book, *The Life of My Savior*, the text for Grade II, all the necessary doctrine has been given the children in an interesting story form. The children are not to memorize the lessons, except at times some Scriptural texts or poems. Through a careful reading of the book, the child will incidentally learn the fundamental religious truths necessary for little children. Practically every question of the *Baltimore Catechism* has been used in the course. These questions have been inserted verbatim, where they naturally belong. Consequently the child will know the questions of the *Baltimore Catechism,* No. 2, at the completion of the second grade.

Warning!

Let the teacher be very conscientious and prudent in asking questions and explaining them, so as never, even for one instant, to place a doubt in the mind of the child regarding any doctrine of the Church. The following case serves as an example of a question capable of creating doubt:

TEACHER: Was Jesus Christ truly God?

PUPIL: Yes, Jesus Christ was truly God.

TEACHER: *But* how could Jesus, *if He is God,* die on the Cross?

A statement like the above, *But* and *if He is God,* is indeed capable of making an exceedingly unfortunate and dangerous impression upon the mind of a little child.

Prayers

The prayers of the children should be few and simple. The main addition to the prayers for Grade II are the Creed and the Stations of the Cross. In the Doctrine Booklet the Creed should be very prominent.

During Lent the prayer of the Stations of the Cross will be studied.

The other prayers are the usual daily morning, night, and table prayers, the Acts of Faith, Hope, Charity, and Contrition.

The Rosary is taught in parts throughout the year as the respective incidents in the life of our Lord and our Lady are studied.

Every child should be encouraged often to say the ejaculatory prayers suggested throughout the Manual.

Hymns

The hymns suggested in the course should be taught during the regular daily singing class. Frequently the children should sing a hymn during the religion hour. At times they should be told to fold their hands because they are singing a prayer to God. They should always sing softly and with devotion. Occasionally a few of the children will sing the words while the others softly hum the melody. Suggest to them to sing these hymns softly in their hearts to Jesus when they visit Him in church; also to teach their little sisters and brothers the hymns they have learned in school.

Poems and Quotations

The teacher should have at her disposal a collection of suitable poems and quotations gathered from year to year for use in the religion classes. Some of the simpler poems could be memorized. Scriptural quotations must be explained to the children.

Some of the poems are intended for reading by the teacher to the class. This may be one method of introducing the day's lesson.

An exercise in drill in Scripture texts could be conducted as follows: The teacher will give the text and ask the class to tell under what situations and by whom it was first said. The children can test each other's knowledge of the texts in this same manner.

Virtuous Practices

The hints for the practice of virtue in the child's life, which are referred to in the lessons, are usually a direct lesson learned from the story. It would be well at times to have the children suggest their own little practices.

Developments

Children must live their stories. The purpose of the developments is to give them the opportunity of really entering heart and soul into the beautiful life of Jesus. Every faculty of mind, heart, and soul of the child must be brought into play, must be exercised through a happy correlation of the work and play instincts.

Purposeful activities, in which, however, the child is permitted liberty of choice, will expand the powers of the soul and often cause the latent powers of mind to become active. The deep emotional nature of the child will find ways and means of beautiful expression, if only the child be given his rightful opportunities. Teachers should not fear a loss of time, for how can that time be lost in which the pupil, through his creative art and expression, lives the beautiful stories of his little Leader, Jesus, in thought, word, and act?

As suggested again and again in the various Units, the teacher need not take all the activities. Many have been noted; it is for her to select those appealing to her and most suitable to her class. She must always keep in mind the purpose of the activity, the coming close to Jesus in love by knowing Him better through every thought, word, and deed.

In these activities let the work often be carried out in a socialized manner. Have the class divided into small groups and seated or standing about informally, telling one another all about the story or about the project. The teacher can quietly pass from group to group and give her comments and commendations, or retell the story to the group. She must be the master hand guiding continually toward Christ.

Creative Song

Perhaps one phase of work which has been entirely neglected in the Religion Classes is that of creative music. Let the children compose their own songs and melodies, and sing them for the other classes. Children sing spontaneously, as can be well perceived when they are at play. Bring the creative-song ability, inherent in almost every child, into play on many occasions. Praise every child for his attempt and tell him Jesus loves his very own song best of all.

Let the children suggest a title for a song that would be suitable for the lesson in question; e.g., at Christmas time the title, "Sweet Baby Jesus."

Then talk over the rhythm, clap the rhythm, tap it, and sing it. Do this until the children are perfectly sure of the rhythm.

Now suggest that the class think of any words that will fit into this rhythm and follow the thought of the title. Let the children suggest one line at a time. Write these lines on the board, and let them choose which they like best. Continue until one stanza of four lines has finally evolved.

Now talk over what expression, soft, loud, tender, will best suit each line and each prominent word. Write this word above the line at the board.

Finally, let them quietly think of a melody of their own which will fit the first line. They will make their suggestions by singing their own melody. The teacher will write on the board in the musical syllables a few of the melodies suggested, and again let the children select which they like best. Continue in this way until the four lines have been completed.

(Adapted from "Creative Music" by Pearl Sanford, *The Instructor,* January, 1932.)

Booklets

Children always delight in making booklets. A number of booklets has been suggested in this course for Grade II. The teacher need not make them all, although they are arranged in such time order that all can be done. As a general rule these booklets should be simple, clean, and neat. The size depends upon the wish of the teacher and the class.

The main purpose of this activity is to impress more deeply upon the heart and mind of the child, the religious ideals to be inculcated by each one, particularly the one prevailing thought of the year: the Divinity and Humanity and Personal Love of Christ for each child.

Pictures, poems, original drawings, quotations, memory gems, and various other devices can be used in making the booklets. The children should be free to go on as they wish, while again the teacher guides and inspires to beautiful work for the love of Jesus.

Dramatization

The work in Religion, Grade II, is very well adapted to dramatizations. The children should be given ample opportunity to express their creative abilities. Dramatization is among the principal methods of self-expression. The children should be allowed their own selection of words, but where the exact Biblical quotations are possible, they should be used.

As a general rule, in the public life of our Lord, there should be no impersonation of Jesus. The events leading up to the moment when the Lord Himself appears can be dramatized. Then a child or occasionally the teacher should continue the story by *telling* or *reading*, not by dramatizing, the actions of the Lord. A scene showing the results of our Lord's words or deeds can be dramatized.

The following outline is suggestive of the above method:

The Healing of the Ten Lepers

Scene I. The lepers are talking about what they had heard of Jesus. Suddenly a large crowd comes down the road. Children, taking the parts of the people, will walk down the aisles praising the Lord. The lepers rush forward, stop and shout: "UN-CLEAN!" The people recoil before them. The lepers inquire what this is all about. On hearing of Jesus, they immediately kneel down, and with outstretched arms, cry: "Have mercy on us!"

Scene II. One of the children or the teacher tells the story of how Christ speaks kindly to the lepers, heals them, and tells them to show themselves to the priests.

Scene III. Shows the lepers pronounced clean by the priests. One pleads with the others to return to Jesus to thank Him; they all refuse and give some flighty excuse. He alone returns.

Scene IV. Shows the one leper returning to the Lord. At a distance he sees Christ and calls out his thanks, and then rushes forward as if to kneel at the feet of Jesus.

Scene V. The conversation between Christ and the leper is told or read by a child or the teacher. The exact quotations should be used.

Programs

The programs suggested in the course are to be very informal, a natural result of the day's feast, lesson, or some legal celebration. Some little touches in the way of clothes, headdress, furniture can be added to produce the respective atmosphere.

The pastor, the Sister Superior, other classes, and parents should be invited occasionally. This will help to arouse and keep up the enthusiasm of the class. The teacher should be sure to keep in mind that all these programs are to be another means of lifting the child's heart to good and holy things. While not forcibly dragging in religion, the religious spirit naturally should pervade each program.

Self-Expression

In creative art, writing, song, and dramatization, a child can be given opportunities for the expression of his religious emotions. These opportunities should not be neglected. Indeed, if we wish a Catholic laity which will assert its rights, which will stand before the world ready to express its convictions, we must start early in the life of the child, giving him many opportunities for self-expression.

Pupil's Readings

It would be most advantageous to have as many supplementary second-grade readers and also first-grade readers in the classroom as possible. Certainly many Catholic readers, recognized by authorities as good, should be at hand continually and the children given free access to them. They will enjoy looking up their own stories, reading them, and finally telling them to the class. All these stories must refer to the unit in religion which is being studied at the time. In the lessons of the manual just a few readers have been noted; it is understood that many more excellent Catholic second-grade readers should be in the hands of the children.

Non-Catholic readers contain very fine character stories which might well fit into a unit in this religion course; e.g., stories of honesty, unselfishness, courtesy. The teacher ought to encourage the reading of these stories, also the retelling of the same in the religion or oral English classes.

One corner of the room should be fitted out very simply for the library. A few small chairs and tables would help greatly in creating a reading atmosphere. The children may be given colored cards on which they can note in a simple way each time they have consulted another reader and have read a story in it.

Teacher's Notes

The space left for the teacher's notes should be well utilized. In it should be noted any improvements, criticisms, or other suggestions that might be helpful either for the teacher herself in coming years or for a revision of this plan. It should also contain information as to the sources of helpful material used, such as poems, texts, pictures, and activities that proved unusually successful. Pupil reactions and suggestions should also be noted.

General

Pupils should be encouraged again and again, after the first few weeks are over, to show the results of their efforts to their parents, to tell them their little stories, to read the stories in *The Life of My Savior* to them, to get them to pray with them, to go to Holy Communion or to Mass with them. Many a careless Catholic has been brought back to the Church through the innocent words of a child.

The lessons in religion should never be a thing apart. That does not mean that religion must be forcibly dragged into every activity of the day, but rather that the whole atmosphere in a Catholic school must be a religious one. In the study of the various units, the appearance of the classroom will help much to create this atmosphere. The setting of the classroom in the unit on "Stories of the Sea," as an example, should put the child in touch with many phases of sea life; and so in every unit.

After all is said and done, the teacher is and always must be the most important factor in the teaching of religion. The more she realizes her exalted position, the more conscientious she will be in preparing herself for the great work of leading the little ones ever closer to the Heart of the God-man, Jesus Christ.

Various Devices and Suggestions

1. *Game of Pictures:* A child steps before the class and says: "I see a picture" then proceeds to explain the figures on the picture he has in mind. The others will guess what the picture is and will retell the story it portrays.

2. *Game:* Children put their heads on the desk and think about a story. When Sister calls a name, the child will run to the front of the room and tell a few things about the story.

3. The children may draw a picture to go with each stanza of a poem they like.

4. Make a list of words suggested by any picture they study.

5. Write on the board phrases occurring in any lesson and let the class make pictures which they see in these words; e.g., the waves were wild, the stars were twinkling.

6. Have the children make a dictionary of words that have occurred in their lesson. They may call this: My Own Religion Word Book.

7. *Game:* What would you have done had you been a bird in Paradise? Let the children ask each other questions like this.

8. *Game:* Let the children make riddles:

> I was healed by Jesus when He was far away. Who am I? (The sick servant.)

> I was with Jesus in a boat. Who am I?

9. Copy all the words in the lesson that begin with a capital letter.

10. *Mental word pictures:* Tell what picture comes to your mind when I say: There was a terrible storm at sea.

11. *Classroom bulletin:* Pictures, sentences, words, drawings, announcements to the children, announcement to definite children what they may do.

12. Write the names of all the things you can see in the picture.

13. Coöperative posters in which every child of the class is working at one thing for the poster. Wrapping paper is very good for the background.

14. "Today is Johnnie's birthday, the day when God gave him to his dear parents. Have you wished him a happy birthday?" Birthday or name-day greetings to each child may be written on the board or pasted on the bulletin board.

15. *Game:* Let the children draw a star, fish, mountain, angel, shepherd, camel, crib, donkey, anything they wish, each on a separate sheet. They will hold up their drawing and ask the others what story they know from their religion class which tells them of a star, of a fish, etc.

INTRODUCTORY LESSON

First Day of School
About Jesus

Sept. 1st Week

To the Teacher:

From the very first day of school in September and continuing throughout the year, Christ should be presented to the children daily as God who loves them more than anyone can love them; who wants them to follow Him day by day; who is on the altar in Church to help them; who watches every step they are taking on their journey to heaven; who is waiting for them in heaven.

Pictures:

The Infant Jesus, The Boy Jesus, Mary His Mother, St. Joseph.

Introduction:

Have the children sing a hymn, learned in their first year of school, to Jesus. (The teacher of the second grade should be familiar with all the songs and poems the children have had during their previous work.)

Presentation:

Dear children, how good Jesus, your loving God, is to you. He has called you back to His own school, the Catholic school. Jesus wants you all, His Catholic children, in the Catholic school, because you will learn much about Him here. Tell Jesus very quietly now in your heart that you thank Him, that you love Him, that this year you will try very hard to learn much about Him.

1

Suggest to the children to close their eyes, to fold their hands, then to say a little prayer to Jesus. Wait a few moments and then continue:

Once upon a time a beautiful little Baby came down from heaven to our earth. That little Child was God. His dear Mother Mary called Him Jesus. Jesus was a sweet little Child, always obedient and kind. Who can tell me something about Him? About His holy Mother?

Let the children tell anything they know about Jesus. Have them recite a poem, say a prayer, or sing a hymn alone or in groups to Jesus.

After this, show them the pictures of the Infant Jesus, of Mary His Mother. Let them talk about the pictures. Call attention from the very beginning in the study of the art pictures, to the beautiful expressions on the various faces, the color, and, if not too difficult, the name of the artist and the names of the pictures.

Close the first day's lesson with any song of religious theme studied the previous year.

Lesson I. My Jesus
Sept. 1st Week

To the Teacher:

Ask the children a number of questions based on the previous day's lesson. These questions serve as a unifying factor between the lessons. At times the children ask questions of each other, based upon the previous day's work.

Introduction:

Review Questions: Who loves you more than anyone on earth can love you? Who is Jesus? Where did Jesus come from? Who was His Mother? What kind of Child was Jesus? How can you show Jesus that you love Him? Who was St. Joseph?

"Let us sing a lovely song to Jesus." (Encourage the children from the very first, to sing softly: it is much prettier and instills a certain reverence in them.) After the song, continue with the following:

Presentation:

Jesus, the little Baby Boy from heaven, soon grew to be a Child just as tall as you. He was like you, but, remember, Jesus was a Child and God, too. Jesus kept on growing, until He became a big, tall man like your own father. He was very good to all the people. Little boys and girls He loved very, very much. He used to put His arms around them, and bless them, and send them away, happy.

One day some mothers brought their children to Jesus. Would you like to know what happened to them?

Tell the story simply. Show the picture, Christ Blesses Little Children, while telling the story.

Explain the word *suffer* and the term *Kingdom of God.*

Impress upon the children that our Lord is the same good Lord today as He was then; that He wants the children near Him now as then; that some day, perhaps soon, they will have Him very close, in their little hearts on their First Holy Communion Day.

Now have the children again take up the study of the picture, Christ Blessing Children. Let them repeat the story with the help of the picture. Help them to use their imagination by asking questions: What do you think this little girl is saying to Jesus? this little boy? What is Jesus saying in answer? Which little child would you like to be? What would you say to Jesus? Which lady would you like your mother to be?

Give an instruction on Jesus in the Blessed Sacrament, stressing the following: Jesus lives day and night in His home on the altar. We cannot see Him, but He is there. He promised that He would stay with us. Jesus is God and can do everything He wishes. He is waiting for us to visit Him in the tabernacle. He stays there for love of us.

"Tomorrow, children, we shall visit Jesus in the Tabernacle. It will be like the little children coming to Him many years ago, only now you are the children. Jesus will be so happy to see you, too. He will bless you, just as He blessed the children on the picture."

Close the lesson with a hymn.

Often during the day as opportunities present themselves, point to the large picture of Christ Blessing Children, and say: "Children, Jesus loves you. Do your work very well just for Him. Whisper to Him: I love You, Jesus. This is all for You."

Lesson II. A Visit to Jesus
Sept. 1st Week

To the Teacher:

The next morning's class should be a visit to Jesus in the Blessed Sacrament. With the children as near to the altar as possible, kneeling with folded hands, say very reverently and quietly to them: "Jesus is just behind this golden door. How much He loves you. Whisper to Jesus, as the little children of Jerusalem did a long time ago: Jesus, I am Your little child. I came to visit You. I love You. Bless me, bless mother and father. Make me a holy child."

Let the children pray only a few minutes. Remind them to have a little talk with the blessed Mother of Jesus, too. End the visit with a hymn to Jesus, sung very softly by the children.

Upon returning to school instruct the children on our Lord's presence in His little golden home. It is called the tabernacle. Inside are white silk curtains. The little door is always locked, only the priest may open it. Here Jesus remains, day and night, praying for us all, waiting for us to come to Him.

Teach the children how to conduct themselves in church. The little boy must be a perfect gentleman, the little girl a real lady before Jesus. Stress the following: to talk only to Jesus and not to any of the children in church; to kneel and stand straight; to recite little prayers, poems, and songs quietly to Jesus.

Practice the genuflection and the prayer to be said while genuflecting: Jesus, I adore Thee; also taking Holy Water and making the sign of the cross.

Close the period by reciting or having the children recite a poem to Jesus which they learned in *The Book of the Holy Child*.

Lesson III. Jesus' Own Prayer
Review of Prayers
Sept. 1st Week

To the Teacher:

A review of the important daily prayers of the children is very necessary early in September. Spend the remainder of the week in this review. Convince yourself that each child is saying the words correctly.

During the week have as many pictures illustrative of prayer as possible about the classroom; e.g., *The Child Samuel at Prayer*, Reynolds; *The Virgin Mary*, Ittenbach; *The Annunciation*, Fra Angelico; *The Guardian Angel*, Oswald. Tell the children to bring any pictures about prayer to be mounted in the classroom.

Introduction:

A hymn to Jesus.

Presentation:

You often talk to your dear mother and father, children. They love to hear you, their little child, tell them how much you love them. They like to hear about your games, and your friends, and even your little sorrows. God is your Father in heaven. He, too, wants you to speak to Him often every day. When you speak to God, you are praying. The grandest prayer is Jesus' own prayer, the Our Father.

Explain each petition carefully but simply. Try to have the children acquire the habit of associating some thought with at least some of the words. For stories illustrative of the various petitions, see *Teacher Tells A Story*, Vol. I, pages 58–78.

A review of the Hail Mary is necessary. Show the picture *The Annunciation*, and tell, or have the children tell, the story. See

Teacher Tells A Story, Vol. I, pages 78–79, for stories illustrative of the Hail Mary. Sing a hymn to Mary.

Review the sign of the cross. Let them make it on the crucifix. Teach them to kiss the cross devoutly. Emphasize the fact that the figure on the crucifix is the same Jesus, born in Bethlehem, suffering and dying on the cross for us. Teach the use of holy water with the sign of the cross. Have them cut out or model in clay a cross. While engaged in this work, they softly repeat the words, "In the name of the Father," etc.

Review a prayer to St. Joseph. Show the children a picture of St. Joseph. Let them talk about St. Joseph.

Review the prayer to the Guardian Angel. Speak of his care and love, his continual presence and prayer for his child. Sing a hymn to the Angel; also study any Guardian Angel picture.

Review any other prayers, especially the morning and evening prayers.

During the above reviews, after the regular instruction periods, have the children look up the stories on prayer in any readers. They will tell or read these to the other children during the story-hour periods.

Finish the week's work with one more reading of the lesson and with the exercise at the end.

Pupil's Reading:

(All pupil's readings are taken from second-grade readers.)

Ideal Catholic, "Why the Birds Sing," page 25; "The Bird's Prayer," page 27.

American Reader, "A Child's Prayer," page 41; "A Little Boy's Prayer," page 1; "Mozart's Prayer," page 147.

Cathedral Basic, "Little Samuel," page 86.

American Cardinal, "How Ruth Found Her Way," page 5.

Misericordia, "A Gift," page 1; "Blessed Herman Joseph," page 17.

Marywood, "The First Day of School," page 9; "Your First Day of School," page 9.

Teacher's References:

The Little Ones, "Jesus Blessed Children," pages 78–80; "The Sign of the Cross," pages 11–14; "The Angels," pages 16–25.

To the Heart of the Child, "The Angels," Lesson III.

The Catholic School Journal, Sept., 1931, "The Angels"; March, 1932, "Ite ad Joseph."

The Public Life of Our Lord, Vol. II A, Bishop Goodier, No. 98.

Holy Scripture, Matthew, xix. 3–5; Mark, x. 13–16.

Teacher's Personal Notes:

UNIT I. THE GRANDEST STORY EVER TOLD

Lesson IV. The Grandest Story Ever Told
Sept. 2nd Week

To the Teacher:

This week's work includes Part I and Part II of The Grandest Story Ever Told. Encourage the children to tell their parents what they have learned during their religion class.

Introduction:

Introduce the story of creation by having the children point to objects on the pictures about the room and also in nature, e.g., sky, sun, trees. Let them repeat the words "God made the . . ." as they point to these creatures. Let them recite any little poems they may know about Nature.

Presentation:

Children, there was a time when there were no sun, no stars, no trees, no birds, no earth, not even a heaven. There was only God. God always was and always will be. The grandest story that was ever told is the story of how Almighty God made all things. Would you like to read the story? It is in your books. Sister will read the story for you. You follow her words in your own books.

Read Part I as beautifully as possible, so as to inspire the children with the feeling of awe for the Almighty Creator.

After this let the children read it quietly. Ask them questions on each paragraph. Have them repeat the story of Part I in their own simple words, orally.

Have them read Part II quietly and then repeat the story.

Let the class, one at a time, read the parts they like best, aloud.

8

After the reading of the paragraph on heaven, speak to them of heaven. For a description see the Apocalypse, Chap. IV. Stress the fact that heaven is our real home, where God wants us to be with Him forever. Also quote: "And God shall wipe away all tears from their eyes: and death shall be no more, nor mourning, nor crying, nor sorrow shall be any more." (Apoc. xxi. 4.)

After the paragraph on the angels is read, relate the story of the good and bad angels. Show the picture of St. Michael fighting the devil (Hofmann). Try to have the children realize to some extent the holiness of God, who cannot permit the slightest unholy creature in His presence. Study any other picture of angels, especially *Christmas Chimes* (Blashfield).

At the reading of the creation of earth, tell the story in more detail to the class. Repeat the creation story by days. The children will start a "Creation Booklet." Suggestions for booklet: The child will trace six large circles. He should be given ample opportunity for self-expression. Short sentences referring to the creation can be written on each circle and illustrated by pictures representing the day's creation.

Stress the *goodness* of God to make all things so beautiful for us.

A visit to a park or to any other beauty spot of nature with the class will present to the teacher immense possibilities of showing the beauty and power of God in His creation. Lift the child's mind from nature to nature's God at every possible occasion. Let children add the pictures or names of objects seen in the park to their Creation Booklet.

Doctrine Booklet: Toward the end of the week let the children write their first doctrinal sentences: I believe that God made heaven; I believe that God made the angels; I believe that God made the world. These sentences should be illustrated with pictures. Let the children give one more oral reading of Parts I and II. Then end the lesson with the child's activity, *Something to Do.*

Part III. The Creation of Adam and Eve
Sept. 3rd Week

Introduction:

Introduce the lesson by telling the children that God still had to create the most wonderful creature, man. Stress the fact that all things were made for man. Now that the earth was ready, God made man.

Presentation:

Once upon a time there was nobody on this earth, not one woman, not one child. The story of how God made man is in your book. Read it quietly and then tell all you know about it.

Proceed as in Parts I and II, asking questions on the various parts: "Read the part of the story that tells how God made Adam. Read the part that tells how God made Eve. Read the part that tells where Adam and Eve lived."

Explain carefully that the soul is immortal. Explain a few more of the details of the story. Make the stories very vivid. Have the children dramatize the naming of the animals by Adam, or any other scenes, e.g., Adam and Eve walking through the garden and admiring its beauties, naming the trees, the flowers, the birds. Always have them end the dramatizations by saying to God: "We thank Thee, our Creator, for all," or similar expressions.

Let them work out the activities in "Something to Do." Different groups will carry on different activities.

Let all the children participate in some way in the sand-table project: The Garden of Paradise.

Creation Booklet: Let them illustrate by pictures or original drawings Adam and Eve in Paradise.

Part IV. God Made Me
Sept. 3rd Week

Introduction:

Start this part of the story with the study of the picture, *The Heavenly Messenger*, by Lefler. It shows the Angel of God bringing to a home on earth a little child. Have the children tell about their baby at home. Place many baby pictures about the room; also some Negro, Indian, Chinese baby pictures. Stress the point that God made them all for heaven, that all men are brothers and sisters.

The children may bring their own baby pictures to school for a few days. The poem "The Baby," by G. MacDonald, might be written on the board and the children encouraged to study it. Read it to the class a number of times with much expression. Let the individual children try to read it.

Presentation:

God loved Adam and Eve so very much. He wanted to give them the dearest gifts He could. In your Religion Book you will see what God gave them. Read the story on page 16.

Let them read quietly. After the necessary helps in reading and understanding, ask questions on each sentence. Have them read aloud the parts they like best. Give a short, simple, instruction on why God created us, using the words of the Catechism as a guide: God made me to know Him, to love Him, to serve Him, in this world, and to be happy with Him forever in heaven. Tell the children how they can know, love, and serve God, giving specific instances.

Talk about their many friends in heaven, the Blessed Virgin, St. Joseph, the saints, people they loved who are now dead, perhaps the parents of some of the children.

Show them the picture, *To God,* by Kaulbach. Note particularly the intense joy of the released soul. Explain the picture to them. After these talks have the children read the story aloud once more.

End the lesson with the activities, "Something to Talk About," page 17. Let each child think a few moments on one statement at a time. Pass from child to child, asking each in turn to whisper to you what he is thinking.

Additional Activities: During the composition class, have the children write short sentences on "My Friends in Heaven."

Have the children find stories in supplementary readers on creation or any other related topic. The oral presentation of these can take place in the regular oral-expression class. A dramatization of these can also be given. Doctrine Booklet: I believe that God made Adam and Eve. I believe that God made me.

Pupil's Readings:

Life on Earth of Our Lord: The Story of the King, pages 10–13.

The Catholic Child, "The Chosen One," pages 1–8.

American Second, "Who made the Birds?" page 23; "The Creator," page 118.

American Cardinal, "God's Outdoors," page 216.

Ideal Catholic, "God's Light," page 9.

Teacher's References:

Book of Genesis, Chaps. I, II, III, "Creation."

The Little Ones, "God Made Me," page 9; "God Can Do Everything," pages 14, 53, 54; "Adam and Eve," page 59; "Heaven," page 74.

A Child's Garden of Religion Stories, Chaps. I, II, "Creation."

Teacher Tells a Story, Vol. I, "Creation," pages 52–68.

Religion Through Art, Book I, "Clay Modeling," page 25.

Teacher's Notes:

Part V. My Guardian Angel
Sept. 4th Week

Introduction:

Study the picture in the text. Have the children repeat the story of the creation of the angels. Tell the children about the good angels. Show the pictures: *The Messenger, The Guardian Angel, To God* (Kaulbach). These pictures will unify the story of the child and his angel from birth to death. Let the class sing a Guardian Angel hymn.

Presentation:

Read the poem to the children in beautiful, rhythmic manner. Help the children to get the meaning. Call attention to the phrases or words which present a "mind picture." Note the words which rime and let the children rime words. Have them select the lines or stanza they like best; and encourage them to memorize any poem they like.

Teach the children the prayer "Beautiful Angel," *Book of the Holy Child,* page 18. Say this prayer at times with the regular school prayer.

Tell the story of St. Frances of Rome and Her Guardian Angel; feast celebrated on March 9.

At this point it would be well briefly to explain the catechism questions on the angels:

1. What are angels?

2. Did all the angels remain good and happy?

Have the children read and discuss the poem, "Oh! My Good Angel," *Book of the Holy Child,* page 18.

Let the children read silently the angel poems, "I Wish I Could See the Bright Angel," "When Little Children Wake at Morn," M. Mannix.

Have the children dramatize any phase of child life in some way connected with the angel; e.g., child at prayer while the Guardian Angel hovers over him; studying with the angel near by. Let the groups select any situation which is appropriate. *Warning to the teacher:* Do not make important any *physical* protection of the angel. There is no ecclesiastical approval of these situations.

Angel Booklet:

The children can collect their pictures and arrange the booklet as they wish. Display these in the classroom; the children can offer them as gifts to parents.

Creative Art:

Paper cutting or clay modeling of angels.

Have the children find in various first- and second-grade readers stories about the angels and tell them to each other in a socialized period.

For other suggestions, see *The Little Ones*, pages 16–25.

Now read the poem again and work the exercise.

Teacher's References:

The Holy Bible, Matthew, Chapter IV.

The Little Ones, "The Angels," pages 16–25.

Practical Aids, "The Smile of Your Guardian Angel," page 13.

To the Heart of the Child, Lesson III, "The Angels."

Catholic School Journal, September, 1931, "The Guardian Angels."

Teacher's Notes:

Part VI. God's Loving Promise
Sept. 4th Week

Introduction:

Have the class repeat the story of the creation of Adam and Eve. This review will be through short questions asked by the teacher. The children may ask each other questions. Stress the love of God for Adam and Eve in that He made all things for them and for their children. Speak of their happiness in Paradise. Then continue with the presentation.

Presentation:

God wanted Adam and Eve to show Him that they loved Him, too. He gave them just one command. If they kept it, they would prove to God that they loved Him. Find in your Religion Book, on page 20, what God wanted Adam and Eve to do for Him. When you know, you may read that part of the story to the class.

After the children have told what God commanded, say: "Now read and find out what Adam and Eve did. Tell us the story when you know."

"When you have been naughty and offended your father, what must your father do to you? God had to punish Adam and Eve, too. Now read and see how God punished them."

"Read the words that God said. What do you think they mean?" (Explain carefully the quotation to the class.)

"The next part of the story tells you what happened to us, too, because Adam and Eve sinned. Read the lines that tell you. Stand when you know."

Explain the word *promise*. "Then God had pity on Adam and Eve and on us. Find at the end what wonderful promise God made."

Study the picture in the lesson. Let the children tell all they know about Mary and Jesus.

Study the picture, *The Expulsion of Adam and Eve*, by Doré. Let the children repeat the story while they are studying the picture.

Sand Table: Make very prominent the Tree of Life and the Tree of Good and Evil. After the lesson on the sin of Adam and Eve, rearrange the table. Represent the barrenness of the world on one half of the table, still keeping the other part very beautiful. Cut out an angel holding a sword from an art picture, mount on cardboard, and place at the gate of Paradise.

Talk with the children about the awfulness of sin, especially big sins. Have the children present little daily situations connected with any part of this lesson; e.g., temptation, prayer, honesty, gratitude. For representative problems, see *Teaching the Ten Commandments*. (Bibliography.)

Close the period with an oral reading of the lesson, and then the exercise, "Something to Tell."

Library Period: Arrange a low table with small chairs in one corner of the classroom; calling it the Library Reading Room. Books suitable for children of the second grade and pictures, illustrative of the religion lessons, should be at the disposal of the children continuously. Teach the children orderliness and quiet reserve in the library. For the preceding lessons have the following books and pages ready for the children and the following. pictures. More can be added.

Pictures: Beautiful pictures of nature, of animals, plants, birds, babies, mothers, fathers. *The Child Samuel at Prayer*, Reynolds; *The Virgin Mary*, Ittenbach; *The Baby Christ*, Ittenbach; *The Angel Guardian*, Oswald; *Christ and the Children*, G. Seignas, and any other pictures noted in the lessons.

Pupil's Reading:

Book of the Holy Child, "The Creation," pages 1–12.

Life on Earth of Our Lord, "The Story of the King," "Adam and Eve," pages 10–13.

The Catholic Child, "The Chosen One," pages 1–4.

American Second Reader, "Who Made the Birds," page 23; "Creator," page 118.

American Cardinal, "God's Outdoors," page 216.

Ideal Catholic, "God's Light," page 9.

Teacher's References:

The Holy Bible, Genesis, Chapters I, II, III, "Creation."

The Little Ones, "God Made Me," page 9; "God Can Do Everything," pages 14, 53, 54; "God Knows Everything," page 55; "Adam and Eve," page 59; "Heaven," page 74; "The Blessed Trinity," page 119.

A Child's Garden of Religion Stories, Chapters I and II, "God Made the World," "The Garden of Paradise."

Teacher Tells a Story, Vol. I, "The Creation," pages 52–68.

Art Education Through Religion, Book I, "Clay Modeling," page 25.

Spiritual Way, Book I, "God the Creator," pages 1–26; "The Power to Know and Choose," pages 26–30; "The Soul and Its Powers," pages 38–41; "God Our Loving Father," pages 42–53.

Spiritual Way, Book I, "God's Image and Likeness," pages 1–51; "The Failure of the First Noble," "Prince and Princess," pages 82–106.

Teacher's Notes:

Review:

The questions of the *Baltimore Catechism,* No. 2, can be used as a review:

Who made the world?

Who is God?

Why did God make you?

Of what must we take more care, our soul or our body?

Was there ever a time when there was no God?

Will God always live?

Where is God?

Does God see us?

Does God know all things?

Can God do all things?

Of what two things is man made (Body and Soul)?

Who was the first man? Who was the first woman?

Were Adam and Eve holy when God made them?

Did Adam and Eve stay holy? What did they do that was bad?

What happened to Adam and Eve because they were bad?

UNIT II

THE SWEETEST STORY EVER TOLD
Oct. 1st Week

The story of the youth of Jesus is divided into parts, each of which will take approximately two days. Spend the entire month of October reviewing and studying the hidden life of Christ.

During the weeks before and the week immediately following Christmas, these lessons will be reviewed.

In the *Teacher's Manual,* the activities marked with an asterisk may be omitted until the review at Christmas time.

Part I. The Virgin Mary

Introduction:

Start this lesson with a hymn to the Blessed Virgin Mary. Review Questions: Do you remember the loving promise God made to our first parents? Why did a Savior have to come to earth? Couldn't even little children like you go to heaven without a Savior? What had Adam and Eve done? How did God punish them? Who would be the Savior of men?

Presentation:

The Savior of the world wanted a mother. He was going to come, a helpless little Babe, to this earth. On page 24 in your book you will find a picture of the mother of Jesus.

Study the picture of the Virgin Mary. Let the children tell freely what they know about Mary.

Thought questions to be written at the board. While the children are reading, it would help their concentration to have the questions before them.

"For whom did the people pray? Why was heaven closed?

Why was the soul of this little girl so holy? What was her name? What would Jesus do soon?"

"Now read the story. It tells you about the little child Mary."

After they have read the story quietly, ask questions on each paragraph. Let them give the answer by reading it from their book.

Suggest to the children simple ways in which they can imitate the Blessed Virgin. Have the children make their own suggestions.

Have the children recite any poem to the Virgin they know from their first year's work. Doctrine Booklet: A sentence on the Blessed Virgin Mary.

End the lesson with one complete reading of the same by the children.

Part II. Mary and the Angel
Oct. 1st Week

Introduction:

Tell the story of the Annunciation to the class. A picture of the same should be studied before the story is read by the children. Speak of the purity, love, humility of the Virgin Mary. Now have them study the picture in their own text on page 25.

Presentation:

Read the lesson to the children in· a most beautiful manner. Let them follow you in their own text. If you notice that some of the children have not followed the story, read it again.

Let the children now repeat the story of the Annunciation. Have them use the exact Scriptural words when possible. With books in hand the children should do this:

"Read the words the angel said to Mary. Read the words Mary said to the angel." Now teach the first decade of the Joyful Mysteries of the Rosary: The Annunciation.

Have the children dramatize the Annunciation. The Virgin, a girl with a veil on her head, is kneeling in prayer. The angel, another child with wings, appears, bows low, and gives the message. Continue this to the end of the story. This story can also be pantomimed, while another child reads aloud.

Review the Angelus prayer with the children. Show them the picture of the *Angelus,* by Millet, and talk about what is happening in it.

Doctrine Booklet: A sentence on the Annunciation.

End the lesson by having a child read the story to the class If others wish to do so, give them an opportunity also.

Tell one of the children to prepare about five questions on this story, which he may ask the class the next morning.

Mary and Elizabeth
Oct. 1st Week

Introduction:

Sing a hymn to Mary.

Review Questions:

What did the angel say to Mary?

Why did God love Mary so much that He asked her to be His mother?

What did Mary say to the angel?

Presentation:

Tell the children about Mary's joy to know that Jesus, the Savior, would soon come to earth. Besides St. Joseph, only Elizabeth, a holy old lady; a cousin of Mary, knew the wonderful secret. Tell them the story of the Angel's visit to Zachary and the heavenly message to Elizabeth. Then briefly tell just so much of Mary's visit as to arouse a desire to know more.

"The story in your book, page 27, tells you what happened in the house of Zachary and Elizabeth."

Let them read silently. Call on the children to read the parts they like; the parts that show a mind picture; the parts that have not been read.

To create an audience· situation, invite friendly criticisms of the readings.

Study the picture in the textbook.

Now discuss the dramatization of the story with the class. It may be divided into the following scenes:

Scene I. Mary leaving St. Joseph and walking through the hill country of Judea, singing and praying.

Scene II. The Blessed Virgin arrives at the home of Elizabeth. Let this be a corner of the room near the door. Elizabeth comes through the door to meet her. She kneels down before Mary, holds out her arms to her and says:

"Blessed art thou among women, and blessed is the fruit of thy womb. Mary, my dear cousin, you are the mother of God and you come to me!"

Mary folds her hands in prayer, looks up to heaven and says: "The Lord God be praised!"

Then she takes Elizabeth by the hand and they walk to the door.

Scene III. Zachary comes in the same door and kneels down before Mary. He shows by signs to Mary that he cannot speak. Mary blesses him by putting her hands on his head. The three walk into the house.

Scene IV. Mary's departure from the home of Elizabeth. Both Elizabeth and Zachary kneel before her for her blessing before she goes.

Now tell this story to the class:

One night after Mary came home, God sent one of His lovely angels to Joseph. Joseph was asleep in his little room. Suddenly the room became bright as day. The angel told St. Joseph that the Savior was coming soon; that Mary would be His mother. The angel said: "She shall bring forth a son: And thou shalt call His name Jesus. For He shall save His people from their sins." Then the angel left and St. Joseph knelt down and thanked God. How much God loved St. Joseph. St. Joseph was to be the foster father of the Infant Jesus. How much Jesus loved St. Joseph!

Study the picture, *The Visitation,* by Albertinelli, if it is available. The pictures from the *Sacred Heart Messenger* can be mounted and kept in view of the children on the bulletin boards. Review the story through the picture.

Teach the Second Joyful Mystery of the Rosary: The Visitation.

Discuss with the children many little home scenes, in which they can show their love for their parents, for sisters and brothers. Kindness, charity, unselfishness, respect, are virtues which could be talked about; however, this must all be done on the child's level. Present little problems which occur in the child's daily life; ask them to be the little judges in each problem.

Show the pictures of the *Angel's Visit to St. Joseph,* by Crespi. Discuss it with the children.

Teach the children to say a little prayer to St. Joseph very often. Tell them how good St. Joseph is and that he loves them and will help them if they pray to him.

Sing a song to St. Joseph.

Let the children repeat the oral reading of the story and work the exercise on page 28.

Teacher's References:

A Child's Garden of Religion Stories, "Mary's Visit to Elizabeth," page 166.

The Little Ones, "The First Half of the Hail Mary," page 86.

The Holy Bible, "The Visitation": Matthew, i. 16–25; Luke, i. 1–80.

Teacher's Notes:

Part III. No Room in the Inn
Oct. 2nd Week

Introduction:

Review questions prepared by a child. Tell the children about the home of Joseph and Mary in Nazareth; about the workshop of Joseph; about Mary's work in the home. Let the children tell about their own parents and their work.

Presentation:

Joseph and Mary were always happy. They knew Jesus, the Son of God, was soon coming to their little home to be their Child. One day Joseph heard some news. It was very, very important. Turn to your religion book, page 29. Read until you come to what Joseph and Mary had to do. Who knows? Read the part that tells you how Joseph and Mary traveled. Something very sad happened in Bethlehem. Who can tell what it is? Read the sentence that tells you what the innkeeper said. What did Joseph and Mary finally do?

Let each child read aloud the part of the story he likes best.

Show the picture *No Room in the Inn,* by Merson. Let them repeat the story with the help of the picture.

"What pictures do you see in these sentences: Mary and Joseph lived in a little house. Over hills, Mary and Joseph hurried to Bethlehem. They went to a stable on the hillside."

Talk over with the children a plan to dramatize the story. Let them select their personnel.

Dramatize this lesson in three scenes:

Scene I. Joseph comes home to tell the Virgin Mary about the edict. Their departure; Mary carrying a small bundle of clothes; Joseph with his staff directs the donkey.

Scene II. The journey. Let groups of children follow Joseph and Mary, march about the room a few times with soft music and humming. Children represent the angels.

Scene III. The arrival in Bethlehem. Some of the children represent the inhabitants; in various parts of the room they stand about talking over the edict. Joseph stops at each group and asks for room. They answer that they have no room. Finally one man tells about the cave. St. Joseph and the Blessed Virgin start for the cave.

End the dramatization with a hymn.

Sand Table: For this lesson, arrange it to illustrate the hilly country; a prominent path leading to Bethlehem; white sheep on the hillsides; statues or figures of Joseph, Mary, donkey, mounted on cardboard, coming down the road. Change their positions from time to time, always drawing nearer Bethlehem, represented on the opposite end of the table; also the cave in the hillside. Let the children act independently in this project.

Part IV. The Nativity
Oct. 2nd Week

Introduction:

Let the class sing a hymn to the Infant Jesus.

Presentation:

Children, you are very eager to know what happened in the Cave. You may read at once the sweetest story that was ever told. It is in your book on page 31.

Now with the aid of the picture in the text or of any other art picture on *The Nativity*, let the children repeat the story again and again. Encourage them to say little acts of love to Jesus in their hearts.

What picture do you see in these words: (1) The stars were twinkling in the sky. (2) The Virgin Mary was praying. (3) Jesus was in the arms of His mother Mary. (4) Joseph adored Jesus. (5) Angels came down from heaven. (6) Mary laid Him in a manger.

After the study of the pictures, describe very vividly the hillsides, the shepherds, the sheepfold, the darkness of the hills relieved by the fire. Then tell the story of the angels and the shepherds.

Children, your book tells you, in God's own words, about this wonderful event. I will read it for you, and you follow the words. Remember, they are God's own words.

After the reading let the children tell all they can about the story. Study the pictures in the book, as also others you may have; e.g., *The Announcement,* by Plockhorst; *The Arrival of the Shepherds,* by Lerolle; *The Adoration of the Shepherds,* by Murillo.

Once more have the children read the two parts of the lesson in relay.

Teach the Third Joyful Mystery of the Rosary: The Nativity.

The children will arrange the sand table to illustrate the cave with the crib. As the stories progress, let the children represent them on the table. Doctrine Booklet: A sentence on the nativity.

Dramatize the coming of the shepherds as follows:

Divide the children into two groups, angels and shepherds.

Scene I. The Announcement by one angel followed by the hymn of all the angels, with the message. These words should be the exact quotations.

Scene II. The departure of the shepherds over the hills to the cave. Some will take sheep or lambs along as a gift. The children also go along. Let them talk about the Baby Jesus.

Scene III. Shows them all at the crib adoring the Infant. St. Joseph and the Virgin Mother receive them kindly. Let the children say what they think the shepherds said to the Infant, to St. Joseph, to Mother Mary.

The following poems are very appropriate for study during this Unit:

A Child's Thought at Christmas—Mary Jane Carr

The Blessed Virgin—Longfellow

A Child of Nazareth—Father Tabb

A Song—Father C. O'Donnell

Like One I Know—Nancy Campbell

A Little Child at the Crib—Father Earls

Jesus Answers From the Crib—Father Earls

Presents—M. Thayer

Creative Art:

Have the children draw any of the scenes they like. Even though these are crude, praise the child for his efforts.

Cut angels from paper of different colors, paste an angel head on the forms, and paste these as a border along the blackboards.

Make a coöperative poster on ordinary wrapping paper including these scenes: stable, hillsides, shepherds, sheep, Angels.

Creative Music:

The children suggest a title for the song, suitable to the lesson in question; e.g., in this lesson on the Christmas stories the titles, "Sweet Baby Jesus," "Jesus, Infant Savior, I love You," would be appropriate.

Other Activities:

The teacher arranges one corner of the room as the stable of Bethlehem. In it she places a crib with straw, in which lies a statue of the Infant Jesus. Statues of Mary, Joseph, animals, are grouped about the crib. An electric light can be arranged so as to produce a beautiful effect. All should be arranged in such way as to remain in the classroom throughout the Christmas season.

Some of the older children of the school, dressed as angels, enter the room very quietly and sing softly, while they group themselves about the crib. They should not obstruct the view of the children. The crib is lighted, the room itself is dark. The angels finish their song and leave quietly.

A Moment of Silence (Adapted from *The Little Ones*, page 46): Tell the children to sit very still, "With feet still, body still, arms still, head still" (Dr. Montessori). Darken the room, turn on the light at the crib. Children close their eyes. Sister says: "I will be Mother Mary. When I call your name, come to the crib and very softly say to Jesus: 'Jesus, my little King and God,' or anything else you want to say, a prayer, a poem, or sing a song to Baby Jesus." Sister goes behind the crib and calls one child after the other, just in a whisper, the room being perfectly still. When all the children are at the crib, another hymn is sung to the Infant Jesus.

The children should be taught to prepare their hearts as a crib for the Baby Jesus on Christmas morning. This they can do by performing little sacrifices, saving their pennies.

Each child can make a crib by cutting it from paper, setting it up in a clean paper box, which represents the cave. He can fill the manger with straw, fine paper cuttings, for every little act he has performed for Jesus. Pictures of the Virgin, St. Joseph, the Infant, can be cut from cards of catalogs and pasted into the box. (See *Art Education,* Book I, page 18.)

As a reward for good conduct the children may step before the crib and recite a poem to the Infant Jesus.

To impress the dearest words of Holy Scripture on the minds of the children, occasionally arrange them into small groups. With books in hand, one child acting as teacher shall ask the others to read as follows:

Read the words the angel said to the shepherd.

Read the words the angels sang.

Read the words the shepherds spoke.

Read the sentence that tells you what the shepherds found.

The Baby Jesus in the Temple
Oct. 2nd Week

Introduction:

Start the lesson today with a hymn to the Infant Jesus. Read the story to the children, telling them that after the reading, they will act out the story. Make the explanations as they are needed after the story has been read once. Study the picture in the text, having the children tell what they like about it, what is happening in the picture, what they would have said if the Blessed Virgin had given them the Baby Jesus to hold.

Presentation:

Now with the class make the plans for dramatizing the story. Let them name the play; state the characters and the pupils who should take the parts; arrange the number of scenes they wish; select the places in the classroom which will be the settings for their dramatization; send out invitations to Sister Superior and any others they wish; arrange for any simple costuming. All this will be very informal and simple.

Suggestions for the Dramatization:

Scene I. Mary and Joseph leaving Bethlehem with the Infant in their arms. A little girl, with veil on her head, will be Mary and will carry the statue of the Child Jesus. St. Joseph walks next to her. All the children in the room, with paper candles, which they have made, in their hands, follow the Holy Family slowly about the room. They may sing hymns softly to the Infant, while so doing.

Scene II. The Temple. When they reach the Temple, Simeon and old Anna meet them. Mary gives the Babe to each in turn. They express their love to Jesus and their thanks to Mary in fitting words.

Scene III. The altar in the Temple. The teacher's desk may be arranged as the altar; the priest, one of the boys, takes the Infant and placing Him on the altar, offers Him to God. Mary, too, offers Jesus. St. Joseph gives the doves in exchange for the Child.

Scene IV. Return to Bethlehem. Similar to Scene I. Mary puts the Babe back into the crib. End the story by singing a few Christmas hymns.

Activities which the children might carry out in connection with this lesson:

a) Discussions on what gifts they can offer to God daily: their hearts, by keeping them pure; their actions, by saying often "All for Thee, O Jesus"; their thoughts, by always having esthetical thoughts. At Mass they offer themselves to God; also make their penny offerings on Sunday for Jesus.

b) Let the children repeat the story to each other while doing the following:

Paper cutting: a candle, doves, dove cage.

Clay modeling: a candle, doves, dove cage.

Learning the hymn: Mary, Mother of God; and the poem, "Gifts," Julia Davis.

Reading Period: Have them look for stories in supplementary

readers; also in *The Book of the Holy Child,* and tell the others about them.

c) Teach the fourth decade of the Joyful Rosary.

Finishing the lesson with one oral reading by the children.

Teacher's References:

Practical Aids, "Poster Design," page 290: How to cut out doves, camels, donkeys, page 270; "The Purification of the Virgin," page 211.

The Holy Bible, Luke, Chapter XI.

Jesus of Nazareth, "Jesus in the Temple," Chapter IX.

Teacher's Notes:

Part V. The Three Kings
Oct. 3rd Week

Introduction:

Let the introduction to this story be a study of the picture, *The Star in the East,* by Doré. The children will speak very freely about it and tell the story as they remember it from the previous year.

Presentation:

One day the Wise Men were again studying the stars. Suddenly a bright light appeared in the sky. This was the star for which they had been waiting.

Talk about the departure of the Wise Men, each from a different country, and then of their meeting in the desert.

"Turn to your religion book on page 36. We will pretend that we are the kings and will act the parts." Prepare for the play by asking questions: When did this play take place? How many characters will we need? Who would be best for the parts of the Three Kings? Who will be Herod? What else do we need? Where shall we have the stable? What shall we use for the gifts? In most cases let the opinion of the class prevail.

Let them dramatize it, with books in their hands, reading from the text. Again let some children do the reading while others do the acting.

Introduce each scene with sufficient of the story to arouse the interest of the class. Then continue the dramatization as described above.

Study other pictures, such as *The Adoration of the Magi,* by Boticelli, Hofmann, Dürer.

Doctrine Booklet: Let the children write their own sentences. All sentences of the children must be very carefully supervised. Illustrate with pictures.

Oral Reading: Select children to read the character parts; one child will read the explanatory sentences. Let the audience (the other children) listen for a definite thing; e.g., the mental pictures for certain phrases.

End this lesson with the exercise on page 39.

Part VI. A Cruel King
Oct. 3rd Week

Introduction:

Let the children sing a hymn to the Infant Jesus. With the aid of the pictures have them retell the story of the Wise Men. Stress the point of Herod's waiting in vain and his terrible anger.

Presentation:

You remember, children, Herod said: "I am the king of the Jews. I will kill this newborn King!" But God always takes care of His dear ones. Read in your book on page 41 what happened to St. Joseph. Stand when you have found it.

"What do you think this picture means?" Show them *Joseph's Dream,* by Crespi. Let them tell about the angel and St. Joseph.

"What did St. Joseph do when the angel left him? Read the part that tells you."

"Find out what the cruel Herod did. Raise your hand when you know."

"While the little baby boys were giving their life for the Infant Jesus, St. Joseph and Mother Mary were carrying Him far away. These pictures show us how the Holy Family fled away to Egypt." Show the *Flight Into Egypt*, by Plockhorst, and *Among the Pyramids*, by Girardet. Tell the children a few of the legends as given in Lux's *Legends of the Infant Jesus*, if you wish.

"Finish reading your story and see what happened to Herod, and especially to the Holy Family." Discuss the Holy Family. Let the children tell how their family might be like the Holy Family. Stress the virtues of the children in the family.

"Now let us read the entire story once more. Who would like to start it?" Continue in this way until the story has been read again, calling upon many to read.

Creative Art:

Let the children draw any scenes of the stories, e.g., desert, oasis, pyramids.

Have the sand table represent the desert, an oasis, the Sphinx, obelisks, palm trees, false gods. Use statues of pictures of St. Joseph, Mary, and Jesus cut out and supported on cardboard. Move these from day to day. While the children are working at the sand table, let them tell the stories again and again to each other. Suggest to them to whisper a little prayer at times to Jesus, Mary, and Joseph.

Tell the children about the many pagan children. Encourage them to do little missionary works.

Appoint a child to have about six questions ready for the other children to answer the next day on "A Cruel King."

End the lesson with the exercise on page 42. Take it orally in class. Encourage them to memorize these quotations.

Part VII. To a Little Boy
Oct. 3rd Week

Introduction:

Let the child appointed the previous day ask his questions of the class. Tell the class the story of the poem, speaking of the many things the Boy Jesus probably did about the house and in the shop. Speak in detail about this, because Jesus is their Model and Leader. Study the picture *The Boy Christ,* by Ittenbach, or the one in the text.

Presentation:

Read the poem to the class, with the finest expression and sympathy of which you are capable. It would add greatly to your presentation of the poem to have recited it aloud to yourself a number of times in preparation; also to have it memorized. While you are reading or reciting the poem, the children's books should be closed. Read it as often as they care to hear it. Then tell them to open the books and read the poem themselves. Let each child tell anything that he remembers of the poem. Help the children with the reading. Explain difficult words. Now ask them questions, which they will answer by reading the words from the poem: "What did Jesus do in the house? Where did He go then? Was He a happy boy? How did He run to St. Joseph's shop? Did He love the people? Whom does Jesus love best?"

A dramatization follows this reading. Have the front of the room arranged into two divisions, one representing a room in the house at Nazareth; the other, the workshop of St. Joseph. The Blessed Mother, a little girl with a veil on her head, is spinning; Jesus, a little boy, is sweeping, dusting, singing; St. Joseph, with apron and tools, is hammering and sawing. While one child at a time reads one stanza, or the entire class reads it aloud, the characters in the front of the room dramatize it. Some of the other children will be the people of Nazareth whom Jesus lovingly greets.

Have the children find stories of the boyhood of Jesus in various readers. They will tell these during a socialized recitation period.

End the lesson with the exercise, "Something I Will Do for Jesus." Let the children suggest some very definite resolutions.

Pupil's Readings:

Ideal Catholic, "The Boyhood of Jesus," page 58.

The American Cardinal, "The Christ Child," page 4.

The Rosary Reader, "Christ Our King," page 208.

Book of the Holy Child.

Teacher's References:

Jesus of Nazareth, Chapter XIII, "The Hidden Life."

Part VIII. A Mother's Quest
Oct. 4th Week

Introduction:

Review with the class the story of the loss in the Temple of Jesus at the age of twelve. Let them tell what they remember of the story from *The Book of the Holy Child.* While reviewing this event, study the pictures, *Journey to Jerusalem,* by Plockhorst; *Jesus Twelve Years Old, on His Way to Jerusalem,* by Mengelberg.

At the part of the story which tells about the loss, make clear to the children that Jesus had to do His Father's work, even though it meant pain and sorrow to those most dear to Him.

Stress the prayer of Jesus while in the Temple; His attention to the instruction of the Doctors; His questions to them; His beautiful deportment in the House of God.

Speak to them of the real presence of Jesus in the tabernacle; how He sees all that we do in church. Tell about the sanctuary lamp.

Presentation:

Jesus was lost to His dear Mother and to St. Joseph. Mary's sorrow was greater than all the sorrow in the world. In your book on page 44 is a lovely poem that tells you of the grief of the dear Mother of Jesus. I shall read the poem to you. Mary is going from person to person, asking if anyone has seen her Child. When I have finished the poem, perhaps one of you would like to read it aloud.

Read the poem. Dramatize where possible while you are reading it, so as to make it clear to the children. Read it again with beautiful rhythm and expression. Explain each stanza simply.

What does Mary call Jesus in the first stanza? (Explain stanza.)

Read the second stanza and tell us how Jesus was dressed.

In the third stanza what does Mary think Jesus is doing?

Read the fourth stanza. What does Mary want somebody to do for Jesus?

What does Mary tell anybody who finds Jesus, about a reward? The last stanza tells you this.

Give a short instruction on how we lose Jesus by sin; how we find Him again by an Act of Contrition and by confession; how great our joy when we have found Jesus.

Derive practical lessons from the story such as: obligation of Sunday Mass; thanksgiving and joy for belonging to the true Church; deportment in church; asking pardon of parents for offending them; obedience.

End the lesson with the exercise on page 45, Something to Do.

Christ Found in the Temple
Oct. 4th Week

Introduction:

The teacher will again read the poem, "A Mother's Quest," page 44. Let the children repeat the story of the loss of Jesus. Study the picture, *The Boy Christ*, by Ittenbach, Hofmann. Note especially the beautiful features. Tell the children that the expression on their face will become more like that of Jesus, the better they become.

Have the children suggest where they think Jesus might be.

Presentation:

Let this story be read in its entirety by the class as follows: a definite part to be read aloud was assigned to the children the previous day. They will have prepared this very well at home with the help of their parents or other members of the family. The children who are to read the parts of the lesson will stand before the class. A real audience situation will be secured by having the other members of the class listen for a definite purpose; e.g., for the sweetest picture they can see in the story; for the words which Jesus answered His mother; for the part they like best; for the part they would like to dramatize; for the part they would like to read aloud.

After this reading, let them express their opinions very freely.

Now study very carefully the picture in the text. Other pictures to be mounted and kept before the eyes of the children during this work and enjoyed by them, are: *The Boy Jesus*, by Giovanni; *Journey to Jerusalem*, by Plockhorst; *Jesus Twelve Years Old, on His Way to Jerusalem*, by Mengelberg; *Christ in the Temple*, by Hofmann; *The Holy Family*, by Mueller.

An entire review of this incident in the life of Jesus may be taken as here outlined:

a) The departure from home for Jerusalem. Use Plockhorst's *Journey to Jerusalem*. This part of the journey is beautifully described in *First Communion*, by Mother Loyola, pages 128, 129; in the *Life of Our Lord*, by Mother Salome, pages 100–102; in *The Little Ones*, page 87.

Speak to the class of the obligation of hearing Mass on Sundays and Holydays; of the gratitude and joy they ought to show for the privilege of belonging to the true Church of Christ.

b) The entrance into the Temple. Jesus' obligation for the first time to go to the Temple of Jerusalem to adore God. Speak again of the obligation of hearing Sunday Mass. Review the proper method of taking holy water and making the sign of the cross, of making the genuflection. See *The Little Ones*, page 89; *Jesus of Nazareth*, pages 92–93; *First Communion*, page 139.

c) Jesus in the Temple. His prayer and offering; His attention to the instruction of the Doctors; His questions of them; His beautiful deportment in the House of God.

Speak to the children of the real presence of Jesus in the tabernacle; how He sees all they do and think; how He looks for them when they are to be in church; St. Luke ii. 41–52; *First Communion,* pages 138–144.

d) The loss in the Temple. Tell the children how Joseph and Mary were in separate groups and how Jesus stayed in the Temple because it was His Father's will. Speak of the sorrow that Jesus felt for causing His parents such grief, but that He had to obey the will of His Father.

Tell them that we lose Jesus by committing sin; an act of sorrow will bring Jesus back into our hearts; speak also of the sorrow we should show our parents if we have caused them grief. *Jesus of Nazareth,* pages 95–97.

e) The finding in the Temple. Speak of the joy of the parents of Jesus, also of the joy of Jesus at again seeing them. Explain the words of Jesus and Mary.

Tell them of our joy when we find Jesus again after a good Confession or a good Act of Contrition, and of the Joy of Jesus at our return to Him.

f) The return home. Tell of the obedience of Jesus, their prayers and conversation on the way home. Explain the quotations, especially "And He was subject to them." Give a brief instruction on the Holy Family.

Make practical applications of these topics.

Teach the fifth Joyful Mystery of the Rosary.

Finish the lesson by having the children read again from their book "Jesus in the Temple" and by working the exercise on page 47.

Teacher's References:

The Holy Bible, Luke, Chapter II.

The Little Ones, "The Loss in the Temple," pages 87–90.

Jesus of Nazareth, "In the Temple Again," Chapter XII.

First Communion, "In the Temple," Chapter XI.

Life of Our Lord, "The Three Days' Loss," Chapter XII.

Practical Aids, "Jesus Goes to the Temple," page 110; "The Journey From Nazareth to Jerusalem," page 111.

A Child's Garden of Religion Stories, "Lost in the Temple," pages 199–201.

Jesus of Nazareth, "The Death of St. Joseph," pages 100–102.

Practical Aids, "Prayer to St. Joseph," page 72; "Feast of St. Joseph," page 215; "Holy Family Poster," page 289; "St. Joseph Booklet," page 294.

First Communion, Chapter X.

Teacher's Notes:

Part IX. Jesus Says Good-by
Oct. 4th Week

Introduction:

Show the children the picture of *Christ Taking Leave of His Mother*, by Plockhorst. Stress the love between Mother and Son.

Presentation:

Children, the Boy Jesus soon became a Man. God had promised that Jesus would show us all the way back to heaven. Jesus was now ready to do His Father's wish. Turn to page 48. The story will tell you what happened one early spring morning.

Arrange the class into groups. Let the best reader in each group act as the teacher. He will help the poorer ones over the difficulties found in the reading. These groups know they are preparing to give an oral reading of the lesson. The Sister will pass from group to group, helping and encouraging when needed. After this preparation an oral reading will take place.

Let one group ask questions on each paragraph of the other groups.

Give a brief instruction on their relations with their own mothers. Model this on Christ's relations with His Mother. Have each child think over the questions in the exercise, "Answer These Questions."

Sing a hymn to the Blessed Mother.

Play the game on page 50.

At the close of this Unit arrange a Reading Party. As a preparation for this, let the children make plans. Let them appoint the stories in the Unit which are to be read; which will be dramatized; what poem will be recited; what game to play; what drawings they wish to make; what songs to sing. Then they will appoint a committee for each of the above activities, also for decorating the room. They may write, under the direction of the teacher, invitations to the Reverend Father, Sister Superior, their parents, to attend their party. The following game can be played: Showing pictures or drawings on a card, the children's own work, suggestive of the Scripture story. The child who can tell what story is suggested by each picture wins the game; e.g., picture of the sun suggests creation; of a baby, my creation; of a cave, the birth of Jesus.

Pupil's Reading:

Ideal Catholic, "The Boyhood of Jesus," page 58.

American Cardinal, "The Christ Child," page 4.

American Second, "The Annunciation," page 19.

Book of the Holy Child.

Teacher's Reference:

The Holy Bible, Genesis, Chapters II and III; Luke, Chapter II.

To the Heart of the Child, "The Beginning of the Public Life," page 59.

Jesus of Nazareth, "The Hidden Life," Chapter XIII.

Teacher's Notes:

Review:

For a final review of the Unit, briefly explain the questions of the Catechism:

Who is the Savior?

What do you believe of Jesus Christ?

Is Jesus Christ true God?

Is Jesus Christ true man?

Was Jesus Christ always God?

Was Jesus Christ always man?

Who is the Mother of Jesus Christ?

On what day was Jesus born?

Where was Jesus born?

UNIT III

THE FIRST STORIES OF JESUS' PUBLIC LIFE

Jesus and St. John
Nov. 1st Week

Introduction:

Review briefly the stories of the angel's visit to Zachary, of the Visitation, and of the birth of St. John. Let the class tell as much of these stories as they can recall from their first year's work.

Speak of the probable visits of Jesus and John, showing the picture *The Divine Shepherd*, by Murillo.

Then tell of his life in the desert as a preparation for his great work—to make ready the way for Jesus. The picture, *John in the Desert*, by Raphael, will help in understanding the story.

Have the children arrange the sand table to illustrate the desert in which John fasted and prayed.

Presentation:

John, the cousin of Jesus, was now ready to do the work God wanted of him. He was going to prepare the way of the Lord Jesus, to tell the people that soon the Savior would be seen among them. John left the desert and began to preach near the River Jordan. He baptized them with a baptism of penance.

One day something wonderful happened. Your religion book tells you what it was. Read the story of Jesus and John on page 53. Read until you find what happened to Jesus.

While the children are reading quietly, pass from one to the other, to explain any difficulty the child may find. Those who have found what happened may stand to indicate this.

Ask questions on each paragraph. Explain the word *suffer* as here meaning to permit.

"Read the sentence which tells you what John was saying to the people.

Read what John said when he saw Jesus.

Who would like to read the words which Jesus and John said to each other? (Let two children read the conversation.)

Read what happened when Jesus was baptized.

Read the words of the grand doctrine, The Holy Trinity."

Now study the picture of the Baptism in the text, and have the children tell what they like in the picture and why they like it. They will incidentally repeat the story in the study of this picture.

Call special attention to the first appearance of the Holy Ghost on earth. Be sure to stress the point that the Holy Ghost merely took the form of a dove, that in reality He is a Spirit whom we cannot see.

Explain the mystery of the Blessed Trinity, simply and briefly. Follow the questions of the *Baltimore Catechism,* No. 2, page 10: *Is there but one God? How many persons are there in God? Is the Father God? Is the Son God? Is the Holy Ghost God? What do you mean by the Blessed Trinity?*

Tell the story of St. Augustine and the angel. This can be dramatized very simply. Also tell the story of St. Patrick and the shamrock.

Speak to the children of their baptism. This is not a detailed study of the Sacrament. Tell them that the Holy Ghost came into their souls and made them most beautiful with sanctifying grace; that this took away original sin which every child inherited (explain the word) from Adam and Eve; that our bodies are the temples of the Holy Ghost; that mortal sin alone drives the Holy Ghost from the souls and makes men lose sanctifying grace.

Let the children work the exercise on page 55, "Something to Do."

End the lesson with one oral reading by the children.

During the day the children may read the stories suggested under Pupil's Readings, and from other readers, and report them to their class during the Oral English Period.

During the study of this lesson the children may rearrange the sand table to show the River Jordan and surrounding country.

Often write Bulletin-Board Notices: John and Mary will place all the readers on the library table today.

Pupil's Readings:

Our Sacraments, Father Kelly, "Cleansing Water," pages 12–25.

Life of Our Lord on Earth, "The Baptism of Jesus," pages 40–41.

Marywood Reader, "The Children of the King," page 219.

Teacher's References:

The Holy Bible, "The Baptism of Jesus," Chapter III.

The Life of Jesus Christ, Bishop Goodier.

Practical Aids, "St. John," page 107; "The Grace of Baptism," page 148.

To the Heart of the Child, "The Baptism of Jesus," page 65.

The Journeys of Jesus, Chapters I and II.

Jesus of Nazareth, "The Banks of the Jordan," Chapter XV.

Spiritual Way, Book I, "I Believe," page 71.

Teacher's Notes:

Jesus in the Desert
Nov. 2nd Week

Introduction:

Carefully tell the children the difference between sin and temptation, discussing with them temptations peculiar to children: e.g., to anger, to stealing, and to lying. Stress the points that you have noticed in the children's conduct on the grounds or in the classroom. Suggest prayer to the Mother of Jesus as most powerful to overcome temptation.

Make emphatic what a real hero any little child is who will not do what is wrong.

Read the poem, "Speak, Little Voice," by M. Earls. Write it on the board and encourage the children to read it often. Explain that the voice of God tells us in our hearts what is good; the voice of the devil tells us what is wrong.

Speak of the omnipresence of God; of the presence of the Guardian Angel.

Presentation:

The devil hates all good people. How much he must have hated the best Man who ever lived, Jesus. One day the devil tried to make Jesus commit three sins. The story which tells you all about it is called "Jesus in the Desert." Find it in your books and read it. Read only the part of the story which tells about the first temptation of Jesus. Then tell the class what that temptation was.

Let them tell the story of the first temptation a number of times.

Go on with each of the temptations in the same manner.

Study the picture, *The Temptation of Jesus,* by Hofmann. Contrast the beauty of God with the frightful ugliness of Satan; God's holiness with Satan's wickedness; ask the children which one they wish for their leader.

Have the children read the story aloud, each child reading the paragraph he wishes.

End the lesson with the exercise on page 58, "What Would You Do?" Suggest and let the children offer many actual situations in the child's life regarding temptations.

During the course of the day, let them find the following stories in the supplementary readers and tell them during the Oral English class:

Pupil's Readings:

Cathedral Reader, "The Old Woman Who Wanted All the Cakes," page 67.

Ideal Catholic Reader, "An Honest Boy," page 35.

Life of Our Lord on Earth, "The Temptation of Jesus," pages 42–43.

Teacher's References:

The Holy Bible, Matthew, Chapter IV.

The Public Life of Jesus Christ, Bishop Goodier.

Spiritual Way, Book I, "The Problem of Fighting Temptations," page 102.

Practical Aids, "A Game without a Fight," page 14; "Fighting," page 74; "Lying," page 55; "Honesty," page 58; "Stealing," page 59.

The Little Ones, "Temptation," page 66.

Journeys of Jesus, Book I, "Jesus is Tempted," Chapter III.

Jesus Tells a Story, Vol. I.

Jesus of Nazareth, "In the Desert," Chapter XVI.

Teacher's Notes:

The Apostles Are Chosen
Nov. 2nd Week

Introduction:

Study one of the art pictures: *Christ and the Fishermen,* by Zimmermann; *The Harvest Indeed is Great,* by J. Untersberger; the picture in the text. Tell the children as much of the story as will arouse their interest. Let them tell what they can about the picture, what they think Jesus is saying to these fishermen. Ask what they would have answered had they been one of these men.

Presentation:

You will find the stories in your religion book which tell you just what Jesus said to these fishermen. Turn to page 58. Read quietly; and while you are reading, look at the picture in your book.

After some minutes of silent reading ask the children:

"What did Jesus want some men to help Him do? Where did Jesus go one morning? What did He see there? What were the men in the boat doing? What were their names? What did Jesus say to them? What did He mean? What did Peter and Andrew do at once?

"Jesus needed more than two helpers. The next part of the story tells you about two other men whom Jesus called."

Let the children ask each other questions similar to the above. Continue the stories of the calling of the different disciples.

Tell only so much as the children can understand easily. Do not expect them to remember the details. For good reference works on the Apostles see: *Christ's Twelve,* by Rev. Mueller; and *Jesus of Nazareth,* by Mother Loyola (Bibliography).

Children, you, too, can follow Jesus. You cannot leave mother or father, nor go out to preach, but you can live holy lives, you can keep the Commandments. That is the only way little children can follow Jesus. Perhaps some day Jesus will call you, too, when you are grown up. Pray to Him every day for this.

Let the children suggest the many little acts in their life that make them like Jesus, through which they follow Jesus.

Assign a definite part of the story to a child or to a group of children. Give them a few minutes to prepare to read their parts orally. The other children supply the audience situation. Have them give friendly criticisms. The child who reads will stand before the class.

Finish the lesson with the exercise, Something to Draw, page 60.

Pupil's Readings:

Life of Our Lord on Earth, "St. Peter's Answer," pages 52–56.

Teacher's References:

The Holy Bible, Matthew, v. 18–25, x. 1–42; Luke, x. 1–12; John, i. 29–51.

The Public Life of Our Lord, Bishop Goodier, Chapter 23.

Practical Aids, "The Child Apostolate," pages 146–154, 232–234.

Jesus of Nazareth, "The Twelve," Chapter 24; "With the Twelve," Chapter 26.

Teacher's Notes:

The First Miracle of Jesus
Nov. 2nd Week

Introduction:

Study the picture in the text; also *The Marriage in Cana,* by Hofmann. Note first the beauty of Christ's expression as He blessed the couple. Next call attention to the wedding couple, to the Mother of God, to the parents of the bride, to the disciples of Jesus. Note especially that poor people were invited to the wedding. (These details are found in Hofmann's picture.) Let the children talk freely about the pictures. Have them tell of any wedding they have seen or attended.

Presentation:

Children, you will like to know what happened at the wedding of Cana. All went very, very well at first. Then something happened which made the wedding people sad. But Jesus and Mary knew how to make the good people happy again. We shall read the story of the first miracle of Jesus. Take your books. When you have found what made the people sad, you may stand.

The children may read the answer or give it in their own words. Then let them make conjectures of what they think Jesus did to help the people.

"Now read and find out how Jesus did help them. Stand when you know.

"Read the sentence which tells you what Jesus said to His mother." At this point discuss with the children the loving respect and obedience of Jesus toward His mother; Jesus is their Leader. Review briefly the fourth commandment.

"What did Mary say to the waiters?"

Here speak about the power of Mary with Jesus. Learn the hymn, "Mother Dear, O Pray for Me." Encourage them always to ask help from the Mother of God, especially during temptation.

"Read the sentence which tells of the great miracle."

Speak about the miracle on the altar at Consecration; of the privilege of witnessing that miracle every day. Start a simple but systematic instruction on the Mass, taking about ten minutes daily until the work is completed. If desired during this study of the Mass, the children may cut out from construction paper the various articles used at Mass. Pictures from religious catalogs could be mounted and named on a class chart.

The children will review the story again and again, especially in connection with the following activities:

a) Make a tile of the scene showing how Christ blessed the water. Steps: Draw the picture on paper. Mold clay or plasticine into a flat mass. Trace the picture on the soft clay. Cut away the extra clay with knife or stick. Make the lines deeper and broader. Let the clay harden. Color as desired. (Adapted from *Religion Through Art,* Book IV, page 35.)

b) Make a poster of silhouettes of the wedding feast, representing Christ, Mary, a waiter, the jars.

c) Paste a picture of Mary in the Doctrine Booklet and write a few "I Believe" sentences about Mary.

d) A Miracle Booklet has been suggested in this course. As each miracle of the Lord is studied, let them work out the booklet as follows: On the cover page have a beautiful picture of Christ with a few appropriate words neatly cut out of colored paper. On each of the inside sheets let them write the name of the miracle studied with an exact quotation; e.g., The First Miracle of Jesus. Jesus changed water into wine in Cana. "What He shall say to you, do."

Illustrate this booklet with pictures.

Close the lesson with the exercise, "Answer Yes or No," page 63. Answered orally.

Pupil's Readings:

Life of Our Lord on Earth, "At Cana," page 44.

Teacher's References:

The Holy Bible, John, Chapter II.

The Public Life of Our Lord, Bishop Goodier, Chapters I, II, III.

Practical Aids, "Obedience," page 41; "Prayers at Meals," page 80.

The Little Ones, "The Marriage Feast," page 91.

The Journeys of Jesus, Book I, "Marriage at Cana," Chapter IV.

Jesus of Nazareth, "Galilee," Chapter XVIII.
The Child's Garden of Religion Stories, page 208.
Teacher's Notes:

UNIT IV

THE MOST WONDERFUL STORIES EVER TOLD

Miracles
Nov. 3rd Week
Introductory Lesson

Pictures:

Christ the Consoler—Plockhorst, Dietrich.

Christ Healing the Sick—Schonherr, Hofmann.

Jesus Cures the Sick—Joseph Aubert.

Lord, Have Mercy on Us—Dietrich.

Mount as many of the above pictures as possible and place them before the children for study during the lessons on the Miracles.

Introduction:

Jesus proved to all the people at the wedding at Cana that He is God. He had come down to earth from heaven to save us all from sin, to open heaven for us. How much Jesus loved the poor children of earth. How much He loves you. Jesus came on earth to help everybody, but especially the poor and the suffering.

Presentation:

Wherever Jesus and His disciples went, people gathered about them. Mothers brought their little children to Him. The children were not afraid but crept upon His knees, brought Him pretty flowers, and loved Him. Jesus smiled at them all, spoke kind words, and blessed them.

Let the children enjoy and again talk about the picture *Christ Blessing Children.* Sister will read to them the poem, "Finding You," by M. D. Thayer.

Some people brought their sick children and asked Jesus to cure them. Just think how happy you would have been, had you been a poor little lame child; then when you came to see Jesus, He would have taken you into His arms. You could have whispered into His ear: "Please, dear Jesus, make me well." Jesus would have said to you: "My dear child, I love you. Run and play with your little friends. You are cured."

But perhaps Jesus would have whispered to you: "My darling, I want you to suffer this lameness for love of Me. Will you do that?" Surely you would have whispered back to Jesus: "Oh, yes, my Jesus, I will suffer all You ask of me. I know You will take me to heaven some day with You. There I will be well and happy forever."

Discuss with them how even a little child can become a hero, for he, too, can suffer much and gladly all that God may send to him. Stress the fact that God loves especially those who suffer willingly for Him and that He will give them a special reward in heaven. Tell the story of Little Nellie of Holy God. See Bibliography. Let the children tell of sick children they know. Here is an excellent opportunity to teach a life-lesson of unselfishness.

Continue the study of any of the pictures mentioned above. In these studies point out the fact that all sickness is the punishment for the sin of Adam and Eve; that God pities and loves the sick and gives them a chance to do penance for their sins and also for the sins of the world.

Give a brief instruction on how sin causes the soul to become sick; on the effects of mortal and venial sins on the soul. God is the Divine Physician of the soul especially in Confession.

Teacher's Notes:

The Centurion's Servant
Nov. 3rd Week

Introduction:

Let this be an informal discussion on what the children think Jesus could do for the sick. Study the picture in the text. Tell the children that the Centurion was a very good man, that a servant of his was sick unto death. Let them conjecture what the Centurion is asking Jesus; what Jesus is answering; what the end of the story might be.

Presentation:

Now let us read the story in our own books.

After some moments of silent reading, let the children tell the story. Ask questions on each paragraph.

Read the sentence which tells about the city of Capharnaum.

Read the part which tells how sick the servant was.

Read the sentences which tell again what the Centurion said he would do.

Read the words of the Centurion, the answer of Jesus.

Read the most beautiful words of the Centurion.

At this point speak to the children about this prayer in preparation for Holy Communion; also its use in the Mass. Teach the hymn, "O Lord, I Am Not Worthy."

"Read the words of Jesus at which the servant immediately became well." Call attention to the divine power of Jesus, who did not need to enter the house or to be near the sick man to cure him; also of the strong and beautiful faith of the Centurion who was only a pagan.

Let us kneel down and say an Our Father in thanksgiving for the true Faith.

The following activities might be enjoyed at this point. While the class is busy with them, let them often repeat the story to their neighbors. Also ask them questions, as you pass from one group to another, about the lesson.

a) Sand-Table Project: Arrange the table to show Lake

Genesareth, hills in the distance, the city of Capharnaum on one side of the lake. Make the scene as beautiful as possible, using trees, grass, boats. Cut out and support on cardboard the figures of Christ, the Centurion, the Apostles, a beautiful house, a horse, from an art picture. The children can be interested in collecting various objects and pictures, which they will arrange on the table to represent the different scenes of the story. Silhouettes of all the above figures could be made and arranged on the table instead of the figures cut from art pictures.

b) Arrange the children into groups, let them tell the story to their respective group, using the exact quotations. The teacher will pass from group to group, listen to, correct, praise, as she sees fit. (This socialized method should be used frequently in the reviews of all the other stories.)

c) Let the children dramatize the story in three scenes, which they themselves have written in groups, each group will present its scene to the others:

Scene I. The Centurion at home with the sick servant.

Scene II. The Centurion seeking Christ and making his petition. The scene of the servant at home will occupy half the stage setting, to show how the servant is healed at the words of Jesus. Sister will read the words of Christ. Christ's person should never be represented by the children.

Scene III. The return of the Centurion to his family. Their joy and their final act of Faith will close the dramatization.

d) Continue the Miracle Booklet.

e) In the English class have the children study "The Helper," by Rev. Blunt.

f) Spend one recitation period on personal applications; e.g., calling the priest in time of severe illness; gratitude; trust in God. Let the children offer their little stories and suggestions.

g) Creative Art: Have them draw any part of the story they wish. For the figure of Christ, always use the model silhouette.

h) Children add to their vocabulary by using the words: synagogue, Centurion, miracle, in sentences orally.

End the lesson with another good oral reading of the story by the class.

Pupil's Readings:

Catholic Nursery Rhymes, "The Servant."

Teacher's References:

The Holy Bible, John, iv. 43–54.

Practical Aids, "Kindness," page 9.

A Child's Garden of Religion Stories, "The Centurion," page 215.

Wonder Stories, "Faith of a Pagan Soldier," page 235.

The Journeys of Jesus, Vol. I, "Jesus Heals the Servant," Chap. V.

Jesus of Nazareth, Chapter 26.

Teacher's Notes:

Jesus and a Crippled Man
Nov. 3rd Week

Introduction:

Describe vividly a person struck with paralysis. Let the children learn a fine, delicate sensitiveness regarding any crippled child in the class. Another wonderful life-lesson of unselfishness can be instilled into the hearts of the others by the presence of an afflicted child.

Presentation:

Just such a crippled man was living in Capharnaum. He suffered so much and had to remain in bed always. One day a wonderful thing happened to him. Your religion book tells you the story on page 67. Sister will read the lesson for you.

After the first reading and discussion, study the picture, *The Paralytic Healed,* by Bida. In the study of the picture let the children retell the story, using the exact quotations whenever possible.

"Read the part of the story which tells what the four good men did for the paralytic."

Talk over with the children the beauty of unselfishness. Draw attention to the many unselfish acts you have perceived them perform on the playground, in the classroom.

"Read the first words of Jesus in the lesson. When do we hear these same words?

"Read the part that tells how Jesus knew even what His enemies were thinking. Jesus reads our hearts, too. He knows what sins are on our soul this minute; He also knows the many acts of kindness and unselfishness we have done for love of Him." Discuss with them the daily acts of kindness in their power to perform.

Point out that the cure of the man's soul from mortal sin was a greater miracle than the cleansing of the body; that Jesus performs this same miracle on our souls when we have confessed our sins, especially any mortal sin, with true sorrow.

"Read how the paralytic showed Jesus his thanks for the two miracles."

Further activities: Arrange the sand table to show a flat-roofed house. Cut out the figures from art pictures or in silhouettes, to represent the multitudes, the four men carrying the stretcher. Arrange the figures as the story develops.

During the English class take the poems, "A Bunch of Golden Keys" (*Practical Aids,* page 25); "Little Things," by Father Faber; "What Have I?" by C. Rosetti.

Continue the Miracle Booklet.

Now let us read the entire story once more. After this we shall write the exercise, "Something to Write," page 69.

Pupil's Readings:

Misericordia, "Our Lord Cures the Lame Man."

Catholic Nursery Rhymes, page 19.

Teacher's References:

The Holy Bible, Matthew, ix. 1–8.

Practical Aids, "The Gift of Health," page 86.

Journeys of Jesus, "Jesus Heals the Paralytic," page 93.

Jesus of Nazareth, Chapter XXVI, "We Have Seen Wonderful Things."

Jesus and a Blind Man
Nov. 4th Week

Introduction:

Picture study of *Christ Healing the Blind Man,* by Bida. Tell as much of the story as leads up to the act represented in the picture. Then continue with the

Presentation:

The story of the picture is in your book on page 70. Read it quietly, then look at the picture again and tell the class what is happening.

Find the two sentences that you can often say as a prayer.

Read the sentence which shows the reward the beggar received for his faith. Read the sentence that tells you how the beggar thanked Jesus.

Discuss with the class the gratitude we owe to God for the health of body and especially for our sight; how we can show this gratitude by never using our eyes to commit sin. Ask them to suggest how they can use their eyes for God.

Let us read the lesson once more. John, read all the parts which tell what is happening. George, read the words that the blind man says. Francis, the words of the people; and William, the sweet words of Jesus. All do your best for the love of Jesus. Step to the front of the room. The other children will listen.

End the lesson with the exercise, "What I Can Do With My Eyes," page 71.

The following activities will add to the interest of the lesson:

a) Sand-Table Project: Arrange the table to represent the hilly country around Jericho and the road leading to the city. Use either silhouettes or figures cut from art pictures to illustrate the story.

b) Booklets: Doctrine and Miracle. Continue the work in these. Let the children find pictures illustrative of some phase of the story or of some application to their own lives; e.g., visiting the sick. Paste these into the books and write the important quotations in the lesson under them.

c) Discuss the following with the class:

    (1) Gratitude to God for the health of body and soul.

    (2) Guarding the eyes from looking upon evil; seeing the beautiful which God has placed in nature and in men.

    (3) At the Elevation to raise the eyes to the Sacred Host and say: "My Lord and my God."

Jesus and the Lepers
Dec. 1st Week

To the Teacher:

During the study of this lesson, review briefly the steps necessary for the Sacrament of Penance, if the children have already gone to Confession. Stress especially the thanksgiving after Confession.

Introduction:

Tell the children about the terrible sickness, leprosy; of the separation from home and city; of the law commanding the leper to call out "Unclean!" should anyone come near; of their sad life among the caves in the desert regions.

Presentation:

One day as Jesus was walking along the road toward Jerusalem, ten lepers were standing at the roadside, waiting for help. The play in your book on page 72 tells you what happened to them. Let us read the first scene. Mary, you come before the class and read all the parts that tell us about the time, the place, the characters; and all that which explains the play. Who will read the parts of the lepers? Sister will read the part of Jesus.

Explain that the front of the room is now the desert. The lepers are seated upon the rocks and the sand, talking sadly to one another. One of the lepers is a Samaritan. The Jews always hated the Samaritan. Now proceed with the reading of the first scene.

Continue with Scenes II and III in the same manner.

After the first reading, let the children dramatize the play, using their books to read the words. Again while others read the parts, some of the class may pantomime them.

Study the picture, *Christ Healing the Ten Lepers*, by Seifert, Hole. Let the children now tell the story of the lepers.

Discuss topics like the following: gratitude to God for the true Faith; gratitude toward parents, teachers, friends. Let the class suggest daily problems in their home, school, and play life for the practice of gratitude. Review the common phrases of courtesy to express thanks. It would be appropriate to have a Program of Courtesy.

Now speak to them of the sickness of the soul, sin. Review briefly the Sacrament of Penance.

Tell the story of the heroic Father Damien, of Brother Dutton; of the Sisters who even today work among the lepers and may become lepers themselves. Show pictures from various missionary magazines.

Continue the work on the Miracle Booklet.

Library Period: During the day the children will find stories in readers which are illustrative of gratitude, ingratitude, politeness. They will retell these during the period or read them to each other.

End the lesson by letting the children read the play once more. Then as an exercise they will write questions which they may ask each other. The exercise on page 74 will be taken orally.

Since this is the last of the miracles of healing the sick, arrange the children for a socialized recitation. They will retell all the stories with the help of the art pictures. Some groups may dramatize the various scenes. Others may make practical applications of the lesson. A chairman appointed by the children in each group will lead the discussion; of course, only simple things are to be expected of these little children. The teacher will pass from group to group and be the directing force.

Pupil's Readings:

Cathedral, II, "Jesus and the Blind Man," page 173.

Misericordia, "Our Lord Cures the Lame Man."

Catholic Nursery Rhymes, "M is for Miracles," page 19.

Teacher's References:

The Holy Bible, "The Ruler's Son," John, iv. 43–54.

The Public Life, Bishop Goodier, Chapter XVIII, "With the Multitude in Judea."

Practical Aids, "Kindness," page 9; "Generosity," page 87; "Gratitude," page 33; "Selfishness," page 147.

A Child's Garden of Religion Stories, page 215.

Wonder Stories, "Faith of a Pagan Soldier," page 233; "The Pool of Bethsaida," page 248; "The Ungrateful Lepers," page 246.

Journeys of Jesus, Vol. I, "Jesus Heals the Paralytic," page 93; "Jesus Heals the Servant," Chapter V.

Journeys of Jesus, Vol. II, "The Ten Lepers," page 161.

Jesus of Nazareth, "We Have Seen Wonderful Things," Chapter XXIII; "Who Went About Doing Good," Chapter XXVI.

Teacher's Notes:

The Dead Are Raised to Life
Introductory Lesson
Jan. 3rd Week

Introduction:

Begin the study of these miracles with questions somewhat like the following: How did Jesus show that He is God? Who can tell some of the miracles He worked? Why did Jesus do all this? Why did He come to earth? Did Jesus come only for the people who lived a long time ago?

Presentation:

Children, Jesus thought of you, each one of you, at all times. He knew that some day His dear little child would believe in Him, hope in Him, and love Him. By all the miracles Jesus worked, He wanted to show you, too, that He is your God.

In all the miracles which we have studied, Jesus either cured the body and soul from sickness, or He commanded the things of nature and they obeyed. Jesus, too, showed all men that He is Master not only of the living, but also of the dead. He, Jesus, spoke to the dead. At once they lived and spoke again. God is the Master of life and death. Only God can give life, only God may take life.

When people die, their soul leaves the body. The body dies and must be buried. The soul never, never, never dies.

God breathed a soul into each one of you when He made you. Some day He will call your soul back to Himself. God made you, and so you belong to God.

Now speak briefly to them of the reward to good people, heaven; of the punishment of the wicked, who die in mortal sin, hell; of the place where souls go who still have some small sins on them, purgatory.

Let the children recite the Act of Contrition. Encourage them to say this prayer every night before they go to sleep, and every time they commit any sin; also to say a Hail Mary every night for those who die during the night.

Stress the points that death is a joy for the good man; that death is just another one of God's wonderful gifts to us, for without it we could not enter heaven, could never be with God and the Blessed Virgin.

Console the orphan children in the class by saying that their parents see them from heaven, and are happy because they are good; they are waiting for them in heaven.

Let the children speak freely during the introductory lesson.

The Daughter of Jaïrus
Jan. 3rd Week

Introduction:

Start the lesson with the hymn, "Holy God, We Praise Thy Name."

Presentation:

One day Jesus was again teaching in His city at Capharnaum, near the beautiful Lake Genesareth. Everybody was quiet, looking at the dear Lord, listening to His holy words, and loving Him more and more. Suddenly a man rushed down the street. Would you like to know why? Open your religion book on page 75, and read the story so far.

Let the children read until they can tell why the servant came. Sister will read the rest of the story in a beautiful, solemn way.

Now study the picture in the text carefully, or *Christ Raising Jaïrus' Daughter,* by Richter, Hofmann, Keller, La Fosse. Have the children tell all they can about it. Add the details which they have missed.

"Now let us read parts of the story again aloud.

"Read the sentence which tells about the happy home of Jaïrus."

Describe to the class the family of Jaïrus, their kindness to the poor; Jesus' love for them because of their kindness and their good lives.

"Read the parts that tell how sorrow came into this happy home."

Speak to the children of sorrows which are often sent by God because He loves us; how we must sanctify our sufferings; even little children have their cross, which they must bear for Jesus' sake.

"Read how Jaïrus went to Jesus for help."

Have the children suggest when they, too, should go to Jesus for help, particularly in times of sorrow in the family.

"Read what happened in the bedroom of the dead child.

"What do you think the little girl said to Jesus after she came back to life? What did her parents say to Him? Suppose you had been the little girl, what would you have done? Do you think you would ever forget how good Jesus had been to you? If you have ever committed a mortal sin and confessed it, Jesus worked even a greater miracle for you. He gave back life to your soul, saved you from hell, and opened heaven again for you. What can you do to thank Him? God does many things for us every day. What should we always say to Him?"

Continue the booklet on the miracles and the doctrine.

Discuss the home virtues which made the daughter of Jaïrus such a happy child; e.g., cheerfulness, politeness, obedience. Read the poem, "A Child's Christian Day," by Rev. O'Brien, and study it with the class during the regular English class.

Have the children read the story aloud once more. Arrange it so that one child reads all the explanatory parts, while others read the conversational parts. Finally, work the exercise, "Fill in the Spaces," page 77. Appoint a child to prepare questions on this lesson for the review next day.

Additional exercises for any stories in this Unit.

a) Children read the stories silently from other readers, retell them to each other in Oral English classes.

b) A sand table can be arranged for each story with silhouettes or pictures.

c) Read *The Making of the Birds,* by K. Tynan.

d) Teach the ejaculations as they occur in the lessons.

Pupil's Readings:

Ideal II, "The Kindness of Jesus," page 96.

Marquette, "Night and Day," page 94; "The Rich Ruler's Daughter," page 157.

American, "Jesus Raises the Dead," page 98.

Catholic Child, "The Sick Girl," page 160.

Life of Our Lord on Earth, "The Daughter of Jaïrus," page 46.

The Only Son of His Mother
Jan. 3rd Week

Introduction:

Have the child appointed ask the questions of the previous day's work. Include the following: "Who has given life to you; to me; to everybody? Why did God give us life? Who alone can take life from us? Who only can give it back? When will God call our soul? Many, many years from now when you are dead, God will say to your body: 'Arise!' At once your soul, too, will again enter your body and you will rise from the dead. If you have been holy on earth, God will take you to heaven."

Show the picture, *The Last Judgment,* by Michelangelo, and briefly tell about the final resurrection of the human race.

Presentation:

We saw how Jesus returned the little girl alive to her parents. Today we shall learn how Jesus proved that He is God by another grand miracle. Read the story "The Only Son of His Mother," page 78.

Before having the children repeat the story, let them study any one of the art pictures; e.g., *Christ and the Widow of Naim,* by Verchil. Make a special study of the picture in their text. Let them speak freely. Give the children interesting details concerning the hired mourners, the musicians, the burial ceremonies. For these details see *Jesus of Nazareth,* Mother Loyola.

Discuss with the children practical applications derived from this lesson: sympathy for others in their sufferings; prayer and the hearing of Mass for the relief of the souls in purgatory; to keep our souls free from sin because one day God will raise us from the grave, either to reward or to punish us. As Jesus saw the sadness in the heart of the mother, so He also knows all we think, do, and say.

Now have some children read part of the story, and others tell the parts they like best. Give each child an opportunity to read a few lines. Then let there be one complete reading, followd by the exercise, "Can you answer these questions?"

Appoint a child to prepare questions for the review of the next day. Let him ask the questions from the teacher's desk at the next recitation period.

Pupil's Reading:

Life of Our Lord on Earth, "The Widow's Son," page 50.

Teacher's References:

The Holy Bible, Matthew, ix. 20–38, "Daughter of Jaïrus"; Luke, vii. 11–18, "The Widow's Son."

To the Heart of the Child, page 90.

Practical Aids, "Confession," page 77; "Purgatory," page 153; "Heaven," page 39.

The Little Ones, "Heaven," page 74; "Jaïrus' Daughter," page 94.

Wonder Stories, "Back From Death," page 252.

Jesus of Nazareth, "Talitha Cumi!" Chapter 28; "Who went About Doing Good," Chapter 26.

Teacher's Notes:

Some Dear Friends of Jesus
Jan. 4th Week

Introduction:

Start this lesson with a study of the picture *Christ in the Home of Martha and Mary,* by Hofmann. Help the children find all the beautiful touches of a happy homelife in the picture. Tell them the names of the members of the family. Have the children describe Jesus, Martha, Mary, the home.

Presentation:

You will like to read something about the friends of Jesus. You will find a lesson about them in your religion books. Read it and see whether you would love them, too.

Let them read quietly for some time and tell what they know.

There are four pretty mind pictures in this story. Who can find them?

Read the part of the lesson that tells you about their home in Bethany. Read the sentence which shows that Jesus loved to be there. Read about Lazarus. Read and tell us about Martha; about Mary.

Tell the children the story of Mary's conversion by a glance from the eyes of Jesus; of her public penance in the house of Simon; of her sorrow; of the sweet words of Jesus about her. Show a picture of this, e.g., *The Feet Washing,* by Hofmann, Nordenberg. Let the children repeat the stories with the help of the picture.

Read the little story about Martha and Mary in your book at the end of the lesson. Now let us look at the picture again *(Jesus in the Home of Martha and Mary)* and tell what you think is happening in the picture. What are they all saying?

Discuss the characters of the two sisters. Let the children suggest how they, too, can be like Martha and like Mary.

Would you like Jesus to visit your home, too? Jesus loves to come into the home of happy, good people. Even though you cannot see Jesus, He is always in your home with you. God sees all that you do at home. Do you want God to see all *you* do?

Show and explain the picture, *Omnipresence of Jesus,* by Hofmann.

Discuss with them the virtues that make a home happy, particularly what children can do to help along. Let the children offer suggestions how to make mother and father happy. Stress here also *politeness* to parents and others at home.

The Bible does not tell us that Mary the Mother of Jesus was a guest at the home of Bethany. But don't you think that Mother Mary was invited by that good family often? Surely where Jesus was so welcome, the Mother of Jesus must have often visited, too. Mother Mary is watching over your home from heaven. Often kneel before the pictures of Jesus and Mary in your home and ask them to bless mother and father and all of you.

Suggest to them to ask their parents to buy a beautiful picture of Christ and one of Mary for their home, to place it in their living room. This will instill the feeling into the hearts of the children that Jesus and Mary are almost members of their family.

Arrange the sand table to illustrate Bethany, the home of Mary and Martha. Show the flat roof where they often watched for Jesus as He came down the road from Jerusalem to visit them.

Teacher's References:

The Holy Bible, Matthew, xxvi. 1–13, "The Anointing of the Feet of Jesus."

Jesus of Nazareth, "With His Friends," Chapter XXXV.

Practical Aids, "A Child's Christian Day," pages 79–83; "Cheerfulness in the Home," page 8; "Politeness in the Home," page 19; "The Happiest Place on Earth," page 23; "Appreciation of Parents," pages 33, 35–41.

Jesus and Lazarus
Jan. 4th Week

Introduction:

Review Questions: Who were the three very dear friends of Jesus? Where did they live? Why did Jesus love them? How did Mary show that she loved Jesus? How did Martha show Him her love? Do you think the Blessed Mother knew these good people? Why?

Presentation:

Tell the entire story to the children, in simple, beautiful language, of the raising of Lazarus, even should it take the entire period. Ask the children a few questions during the development of the long story, so as to keep them alert and interested. After you have finished, show them the picture, *The Raising of Lazarus*, by Rubens. Let them study the picture in their text also. Note the various details of the figures. Have the children repeat the story with the help of questions on the picture.

"Children, in your books is a play about Lazarus. Would you like to read it now? Let us read Scene I and talk about it. Who will read the explanations? Who will be Mary? Lazarus? Martha? Sister will read the words of Jesus this time."

After the first scene has been thoroughly understood, read the second in the same manner. Let different children read the parts in each scene. Explain before the reading any difficult words or Scriptural texts. Continue this way with all the scenes.

Now go back once more to Scene III. Explain more in detail the meaning of the beautiful quotations. Develop the two articles of the Creed, "I believe in the resurrection of the body and in life everlasting" and "from thence He shall come to judge the living and the dead." In this connection study the picture, *The Last Judgment*, by Michelangelo. Explain in a simple instruction the Last Judgment, the time when we all will be called by Jesus from the dead, to be rewarded or punished for our life.

Study with the children the exercise on page 87.

Have them memorize the three quotations:

"Lord, if Thou hadst been here, my brother had not died."

"I am the **Resurrection and the Life**," etc.

"Lord, I believe that Thou art Christ, the Son of the Living God."

Continue the Miracle Booklet and the Doctrine Booklet. In the latter write the two articles of the Creed mentioned above.

During this lesson the children again can arrange the sand table in two divisions; one half will illustrate Bethany, the home of Mary and Martha. Show the flat roof and arrange as in the preceding lesson. The other half may illustrate the tomb of Lazarus.

Teacher's References:

The Holy Bible, "The Anointing," Matthew, xxvi. 1–13; "The Raising of Lazarus," Luke, x. 38–42; "The Raising of Lazarus," John, xxviii.

Jesus of Nazareth, "With His Friends," Chapter XXXV.

The Public Life, Bishop Goodier, Chapter 31.

The Little Ones, "Martha and Mary," pages 106–108, page 149.

Practical Aids, "Child's Christian Day," pages 79–83; "Cheerfulness in the Home," page 8; "Politeness in the Home," page 19; "Happiest Place on Earth," page 23; "Appreciation of Parents," page 33; "Obedience to Parents," pages 35–41.

Holy Scripture, "The Farewell Supper at Bethany," Matthew, xxvi. 6–13; Mark, xiv. 3–9.

Teacher's Notes:

Review Questions From the Catechism:
1. When will Christ judge us?
2. What is hell?
3. What is purgatory?
4. What is heaven?

UNIT V

STORIES OF THE SEA

A Wonderful Fishing Trip
Feb. 1st Week

Introduction:

Review Questions: Whom did Jesus choose for His companions? How did they earn their living? Where did the Apostles live? Who remembers some of the names of the Apostles? Continue with informal questions on any little fishing excursion the children themselves have enjoyed with their parents. Let them speak freely. Then continue with the

Presentation:

The disciples always liked to fish in Lake Genesareth. At times, however, they did not catch many. The story tells you about one of the fishing trips Jesus made with His disciples. Read it and tell what you remember about it.

During the moments of silent reading, the teacher will pass from child to child, giving help whenever needed.

Read the part of the story you like best.

Read the part which tells about the miracles.

Read the sentence that tells how many fish were caught.

Discuss the fact that Christ again proved His Divinity by His power over nature.

Read the most important part; the most exciting part, the most beautiful part.

Read the part that tells you how the disciples felt.

Stress here the emotions of awe and fear as they realized more fully that God was so near to them; of humility and love, especially that of Peter.

Read the part which shows the kindness of Jesus.

Read the last words of Jesus.

Explain to the class what Jesus meant by these words; that today Christ still calls some to be fishers of men, the priests of the Catholic Church. Let the children suggest how even they can be to some degree fishers of men by their help in winning souls through prayer, almsgiving for the Missions, for the poor, by trying to get Catholic children they know to attend the Catholic school.

Study the art picture in the text or *The Draught of Fishes*, by Doré, Raphael.

After the above discussions have the class continue the booklet on Miracles.

Write these phrases on the board and have the children draw the pictures they see: the bright blue sea; many fish filled the net; Peter's **boat.**

Arrange the sand table to illustrate the lake scene. Let them bring a sailboat or make one to be used on the table.

Work the exercise on page 90, "Find the Right Ending" lesson.

End the lesson with a final reading of the story. Let one child read all the explanatory parts, while the others read the words of the various characters.

Encourage them to tell the story to their parents.

A Storm on the Sea
Feb. 1st Week

Introduction:

Review Questions: What did most of the Apostles do to earn their living? Do you think they knew how to manage a boat? Has your father a boat? (Let them tell about their boats.) Is it easy to sail a boat? Have you ever seen a big storm on the lake? (Let them tell their experiences.) The Lake Genesareth, in which the Apostles fished, sometimes had terrible storms. Today we are going to watch one of those fearful storms **on this lake.**

Show them pictures of ocean waves; e.g., *The Breakers.*

Presentation:

"Jesus had been preaching all day and healing the sick. It was getting late. The next day Jesus wanted to be in a city across the lake. He stepped into Peter's boat and soon they were sailing over the waters. Jesus was very, very tired. Your religion book tells you what happened in this night. The story is on page 91. When you have found what the Apostles asked Jesus, stand. What do you think Jesus did? Read the story and see if you are right."

Study the picture in the text; also *Stilling the Tempest,* by Doré; or *Peace, Be Still!* by Dietrich. Note the majesty of Christ, the brilliant light surrounding Him; the fear and the pleading expressions of the Apostles; the wild waves; the sinking ship. Let them study the picture in all its details.

"There are five mind pictures in this story. Can you find them and read them?"

Read the part of the lesson which the pictures show us.

Read that sentence which tells about the fear of the Apostles.

Read that part that tells about the storm.

Read the sentences which tell of the great miracle.

Jesus shows He is God of nature by commanding the storm, and it ceased. Read the prayer of the disciples to Jesus.

Even little children have many little storms or trials of life, such as sickness, poverty, temptation. If they call: "Jesus, save me!" Jesus will always help.

Read the sentence which shows that God is always present.

Stress the omnipresence of God. Children need this instruction frequently. Talk about the protection and care of God for us in times of danger, if we pray and trust in Him. Study the ejaculation: Sacred Heart of Jesus, I trust in Thee.

Spend a period discussing with the class practical applications of the lesson; e.g., prayer, trust in God, reverence in the presence of Jesus in the Eucharist.

End the lesson with one loud reading by the teacher and with the exercise, "Something to Do."

Jesus Walks on the Sea
Feb. 2nd Week

Introduction:

Describe in detail the second storm; the terrible fear of the Apostles, much more terrible this time because Jesus was not in the boat with them. Jesus was praying on the mountain. He knew what was happening to the disciples. Speak again of the omnipresence and the omniscience of God. Tell the story of how the Apostles were clinging to the ropes, to the broken masts, to the sides of the boat. At this point of the story, let them read quietly the story in their own books.

Presentation:

After the children have read the story quietly, the teacher will read it aloud to them in a very beautiful way, while the children follow the words in their own books.

Now study the picture, in the text, or the art picture, *Jesus Walks on the Sea*, by Plockhorst. Let them repeat the details of the story as seen in the picture.

Ask questions on each paragraph:

"Where was Jesus? What was He doing?"

Have the children repeat their night prayer. Stress the Act of Contrition to be said before going to bed.

"Why did the Apostles sail at this time of the night?"

Speak of the ready obedience children owe to their parents and teachers even in hard things. The harder the thing commanded, the more love they show God and their parents by obeying willingly. Let them tell some hard things they often must do.

"Why were the Apostles so very much afraid?"

Speak to them of always keeping Jesus in their heart by never committing mortal sin. This alone drives Him from us. When we are in the state of grace, nothing whatever should frighten us, because God is with us.

How were the Apostles calmed?

After we have gone to confession, when the priest forgives our sins, let us never be afraid again. Jesus is with us.

Why did Peter begin to sink?

No matter what happens to us, if we are good, God will always help us. Speak of trust in God. Make an Act of Hope in God.

Why was Jesus sad?

Jesus is sad when we commit sin and forget all about Him; also when we complain in sickness, in sorrow.

Why did Jesus work these miracles?

Jesus' love for us is shown in many ways. Let them suggest how God shows His love for us. We must return His love by never sinning.

Repeat the Act of Charity.

What prayer did the Apostles say when Jesus came into the boat?

Repeat the Act of Adoration. Encourage them to say these Acts daily.

(In all the above discussions be sure to let the children give their opinions freely and to offer their own problems and experiences.)

Read the entire story aloud in class in relay. After this, let the children work the exercise, "A Game With Your Friend."

Finish the Miracle Booklets and exhibit them in the classroom.

Take the review test orally. Let the children repeat the stories in which the quotations occur. As a game or contest, groups will vie with each other.

Pupil's Readings:

Marquette, "The Storm," page 79.

Teacher's References:

The Holy Bible, Matthew, Chapter XIV.

Practical Aids, "Obedience," page 38.

The Little Ones, "The Draught of Fishes," page 98; "The Storm at Sea," page 108.

Teacher Tells a Story, Vol. I, "Omnipresence and Omnipotence of God," page 88.

Journeys of Jesus, Vol. I, "Draught of Fishes," page 82; "Storm at Sea," page 151.

Jesus of Nazareth, Chapter XXII.

Teacher's Notes:

UNIT VI

JESUS' STORY HOUR

The Good Shepherd
Feb. 2nd Week

To the Teacher:

A booklet on the Parables is suggested in the course to be made by the children. This may consist in original drawings illustrative of some phase of the story. Do not expect perfect drawings. Give the children the opportunity of expressing their imagination in creative art. Praise them for every drawing at which they have worked conscientiously, even though in itself it is not very praiseworthy. Instead of original drawings, pictures may be used and the story or a quotation from the respective parables be written under each.

Introduction:

No matter where Jesus went, the poor, the sick, the humble always followed Him. They loved to listen to His words. He told them about God and heaven. Sometimes He would tell them beautiful stories to make them understand better how much God, their Father in heaven, loved them. Would you like to hear Jesus' stories? These stories are called the Parables of Jesus.

Show the picture *Jesus Preaching to the People;* let the children imagine they are among the listeners.

Presentation:

Tell the story of the Good Shepherd (John x. 10–16) in simple, attractive language, using the beautiful quotations whenever possible and explaining them to the children. Tell about the love

76

of the Good Shepherd for all His sheep; how the hireling (hired servant) cares for the money only and will run away when he sees the wolves or thieves coming; how the shepherd will fight to protect His sheep.

Now let us turn to our lesson on the Good Shepherd, page 98. Jesus called Himself the Good Shepherd. All the words in your lesson are Jesus' very own words. Read them and tell the class what you think Jesus meant.

What does Jesus mean when He says: I know Mine and Mine know Me?

What do you think Jesus meant by other sheep?

What does Jesus want to do with these other sheep?

What will happen when all the sheep will belong to Jesus?

Can you help Jesus find the other sheep?

An interpretation of the parable may be as follows: The Good Shepherd is Jesus; the sheepfold, the Catholic Church; men, women, and children are the lambs; the bishops are the sheep; those belonging to the sheepfold are the Catholics; those not, are non-Catholics; Jesus loves all and wants them to come into the rich pastures of the Catholic Church. Some day the good sheep will be taken into the everlasting pastures of heaven.

Let the children recite any poem they know from their first-grade work about the Good Shepherd. Have them repeat the story of the shepherds at the crib. This is to stress the fact that shepherds representing the poor, were special friends of Jesus. Show the children pictures of shepherds, sheep, sheepfolds. Let them tell what they know from their own journeys into the country.

Study the picture *The Good Shepherd,* in the text; or Plockhorst's.

Let the children arrange the sand table to illustrate the sheepfold in the hills about Nazareth. Arrange the tents, the shepherd, the sheep, the fires along the hillsides attractively. Also show wild animals and robbers in the distance. Have the children change the position of the figures from time to time. A picture of *Christ the Good Shepherd* cut out of an art picture, will stand guard over all.

Suggest to the children that they, too, can be helpful in some missionary activity through which they can help to bring other sheep into the fold.

Discuss with them how they can be the shepherds of their thought. Every good thought is a beautiful white lamb which they can offer to Jesus. Every bad thought is a naughty sheep which the thief, the devil, wants. Jesus will love them much if they permit only good thoughts in their minds.

(A good thought may be a thought of love of neighbor, of friendliness, a short prayer, a thought of the Blessed Virgin. A bad thought may be one of unkindness, selfishness, anger.)

Children can also be the shepherds of their smaller sisters and brothers and of their playmates. This they may do by keeping them from sin, by teaching them little acts of virtue.

End this lesson with the memorization of the quotations.

The Lost Sheep
Feb. 3rd Week

Introduction:

Show the children again the picture of the Good Shepherd; let them give the quotations of the previous lesson. Who is the Good Shepherd? What does He do for His sheep? Has He any other sheep? Who are the sheep? Who are the lambs?

Presentation:

Jesus told a beautiful story one day about a lost sheep. Would you like to read it? It is in your book on page 99.

Let the children read quietly. Pass from one to the other, asking simple questions on the part the child happens to be reading at the time.

After all have read the story, study the picture of the Good Shepherd with the lost lamb on His shoulder. Let the children tell any part of the story they like.

Ask them what they think the story means. Let them express

their thoughts freely. Then make the application somewhat as follows: Jesus is the Good Shepherd. I am His little lamb. When I am naughty and commit sin, especially a big sin, I run away from Jesus. Jesus is sad and looks for me. I am unhappy because I have been very naughty. Jesus follows me all the time through my conscience. He tells me He will forgive me and will take me back to Himself. I go to Confession and whisper to Jesus: "Jesus, O pardon me, I am so sorry." Jesus forgives me and, like the little lamb, presses me close to His Sacred Heart. I am Jesus' little lamb again! I will promise never, never to commit sin again. Jesus is so happy He tells all His friends, the Blessed Virgin, the saints, that I am His dear little lamb again.

Have the children develop the story on the sand table. One group at a time can be busy at the table, while other groups do the following:

Creative Writing: Write a conversation between the Good Shepherd and His naughty sheep; between the Good Shepherd and His good sheep.

Dramatization: Select groups to write and act the different scenes. Invite other classes to witness the play.

Creative Song: Select a theme for this song: "I am Jesus' little lamb."

Paper Cutting: Sheep, shepherds, wild animals, sheepfold, in silhouettes. These may be mounted for a poster.

Hymn: Teach the hymn, "Jesus Tender Shepherd."

During the English class take the poems, "Sheep and Lambs," by K. Tynan; "I Am the Shepherdess of My Thoughts," by Alice Meynell. Let the children find poems on the Good Shepherd, on sheep, and read them to the others.

End this lesson with another oral reading and the exercise, "Something to Do," page 102.

Appoint a child to prepare questions on these two lessons which he may ask the class as the introduction for the next recitation.

Continue the Parable Booklet.

Pupil's Readings:

Excelsior, II, "I Will Follow Thee," Sadlier.

Marquette, "The Lamb," Wm. Blake, page 52; "The Lost Lamb," page 52.

Every Child, "The Good Shepherd," page 58.

The Cardinal Reader, "The Good Shepherd," page 154.

Corona Reader, "The Tender Shepherd," page 182.

Teacher's References:

The Holy Bible, Luke.

Journeys of Jesus, Vol. II, "The Good Shepherd," page 75.

Jesus of Nazareth, "The Good Shepherd," pages 281–284.

Teacher's Notes:

The Good Samaritan
Feb. 3rd Week

Introduction:

God has given us many wonderful commandments. If we obey them, He will one day take us to heaven. The two greatest commandments are: "Thou shalt love the Lord thy God with thy whole heart and soul"; and, "Thou shalt love thy neighbor as thyself."

We love God when we do not commit sin. How can we show our love for our neighbor? (Let the children suggest ways.) Jesus Himself told another parable to show us how to love our neighbor.

Presentation:

One day Jesus was preaching to the people. A lawyer asked

Him a question. Let us read from our book what this question was.

Read what the lawyer asked and what Jesus said to him. Now who can tell the class?

Because of this question of the lawyer, Jesus told another grand story. Let us read the story quietly. There are three parts to the story. Read only the first part which tells about a priest.

Ask the children questions somewhat like the following: What was a certain man doing? What city was he leaving? Where did he want to go? Who were hiding in the mountains? What did they do when the man came near them? What shows that they were very wicked men? Who came on this same road a little while later? Did he help the poor man?

Now we shall read the second part of the story. Another man passed the same way. Read and see whether or not he helped the poor man. (Explain the term *Levite.*) Ask questions on this second part.

Now we shall have the third part of the story. Something beautiful happened this time. Read it. (Explain the word *Samaritan.*) Again ask questions on this part of the story.

Jesus asked the lawyer a question now. Read the last part of your lessons to see what Jesus said to the lawyer. Explain the quotation, "He that showed mercy unto him."

We shall read the entire story once more. George, you step to the side of the room and read about Jesus and the lawyer. John, read about the Jewish priest; Thomas, about the Levite; Fred, about the Samaritan. John and Fred, come to the front of the room to read. George will read the very last part of the story about Jesus and the lawyer again.

Study the picture, *The Lawyer's Question.* Who are in the picture? Which one is Jesus? Which one the lawyer? What is a lawyer? What is the lawyer asking Jesus? What is Jesus saying to the lawyer? What grand parable did Jesus tell the lawyer and all the people who were listening?

Study the picture *The Good Samaritan,* by Doré, Plockhorst. While so doing, let the children repeat the story again and again.

Let us read the story once more today. Would you like to play it?

Arrange the class into five groups. Let each group write one scene and also present it to the others. Arrange as follows:

Scene I. The man coming from Jerusalem to Jericho; the preparations of the robbers, and their attack.

Scene II. The Jewish priest passing by, stops, looks at him, shakes his head and passes on. Let the child say what he thinks the priest said to himself.

Scene III. The Levite passes by. (Similar to Scene II.)

Scene IV. The Good Samaritan and the wounded man.

Scene V. Arrival at the inn; the conversation between the innkeeper and the Samaritan; the gratitude of the poor man; the departure of the Samaritan.

Have the children present their play to other people.

Spend a period in discussing the following situations: Problems of unselfishness through kindness to sisters and brothers; to classmates, to the poor and the needy, to strangers. Discuss problems on kind deeds for love of Jesus.

During the Oral English class, study the poems; "My Neighbor," Tabb; "The Helper," Rev. Blunt; "A Useful Lesson," Rev. Russell, S.J. Let the children find poems and stories on kindness in other readers and tell them to the class.

Close the lesson on the Good Samaritan with one more reading and the exercise, page 104.

The Pharisee and the Publican
Feb. 4th Week

Introduction:

Review Questions: What are the stories of Jesus called? Did Jesus like to tell the people stories? Why did He tell them stories? What stories did He tell them? (Let the children very briefly tell the parables they have had.)

Presentation:

Tell the children the story of the Pharisee and the Publican. Then study any picture of the parable with them.

Let them dramatize the play, selecting their own characters, planning the settings, and any appropriate or suggestive garment. While one party dramatizes the play, the rest shall read the words from their text.

Give a short instruction on humility and devout prayer; prayers should be said not merely with the lips but from the heart. In this instruction, talk about practical situations regarding humility, vanity, pride, selfishness.

Explain carefully the last quotation of Christ and any other they may not quite understand.

Teach the ejaculation: "Jesus, meek and humble of heart, make my heart like unto Thine."

Study the poem, "The Lowest Place," Christine Rosetti.

End the lesson with the exercise on page 106, "Answer These Questions."

The Rich Man and Lazarus
Feb. 4th Week

Introduction:

Review Questions: Which one of the stories told by Jesus describes a proud man and a humble man? Can you tell the story again? What did Jesus say about the prayer of the proud man? What did He say about the humble man's prayer? When are we proud? When are we humble? What do you want Jesus to say about your prayers?

Presentation:

Jesus was again preaching to the people. He told them a story about a wicked, rich man, and about a good, poor man. You will find the story in your readers on page 107. The rich man's name was Dives. The poor man's name was Lazarus. Now let us read what happened to these two men.

Read the first two sentences. How was the rich man dressed?

Read the sentence about Lazarus. Where did he sit? Why did he stay there? Did the rich man give him anything to eat?

Something terrible happened to Dives. Read the next part of the story. It tells us what it was.

Now read what happened to Lazarus. Where did Lazarus go? (Explain the terms *Abraham's bosom*, *Limbo*, where all the just of the Old Testament were waiting for the Redeemer.) Where did Dives have to go? Why do you think this happened? Was it just because Dives was so rich?

The rich man was in great pain. Read what he wanted Father Abraham to have Lazarus do for him. What did Father Abraham say to Dives? Why did he say this?

Read the last sentence. Why will Dives be unhappy? Why will Lazarus be happy?

What do you think Jesus wanted to teach us all through this story of the Rich Man and Lazarus?

Now let us read the entire story. Who will start it?

Call upon one child after the other, until the story has been read a few times. Then have the children ask each other questions on the story.

Let us say a prayer that God will one day take us and our dear parents and all the family and all our friends to heaven with Him.

End the lesson with the exercise, "Something to Write," page 108.

The Prodigal Son
March 1st Week

Introduction:

Review Questions: What is a parable? What parables do you remember? What did Jesus want the people to learn from His parables? Does He want you to learn from them, too?

What have you learned from the parable of the Good Shepherd? the Lost Sheep? the Good Samaritan? the Rich Man and Lazarus?

Today we are going to hear one more parable. It is about a young man who did not want to stay at home with his good father any longer.

Presentation:

Relate the story of the Prodigal Son in simple, attractive words, adhering wherever possible to the Scriptural text. Dwell especially on the grief of the father at the departure of the son. Show how his father watched every day for his son's return. Give all the necessary details. Let the children ask questions.

At the end of the recital of the story, show them the picture *The Prodigal Son,* by Molitor, Doré. Have them study the picture of the text carefully. They will repeat the story with the aid of the pictures. They may also dramatize the picture.

Our religion book has a little play called "The Prodigal Son." Find it, read it carefully. Who would like to read all the parts that explain what is happening? Who will read the Father's part? the Prodigal Son's part? the Elder Son's part?

After the parts have been appointed, let these children come to the front of the class and read.

Tomorrow we shall play the story of the Prodigal Son. Who should be the Father? (Let the children suggest the various characters.)

On the following day let those selected by the children present the play. They may use their books, or they may give the scenes in their own words. The characters should wear something suggestive.

Let different groups play individual scenes among themselves in various parts of the room. Then each group will present its scene to the others. They may also play it before the third grade.

A pantomime would also be very interesting.

Today let us see what Jesus wished to teach us in this beautiful story.

The story of the Prodigal lends itself admirably to a comparison with the Sacrament of Penance. Explain it in this connection as follows: A parallelism between

The Parable

1. The Father
2. The Prodigal
3. The Prodigal's thought of leaving home
4. The Prodigal's departure
5. The misery of his soul and body
6. The Prodigal's thought of home
7. "I will arise and go to my father's house," and his sorrow
8. "Father, I have sinned"
9. "Make me as one of your hired servants"
10. The Father's reception of his son
11. The joy and the feast
12. Now give a thorough instruction on the sacrament of penance

and

The Sacrament of Penance

1. GOD
2. The sinner
3. Temptation
4. Sin
5. Terrible condition of the soul in sin
6. Examination of conscience
7. Contrition and firm resolve
8. Confession
9. Willingness to amend
10. Forgiveness: I absolve thee in the name of the Father, etc.
11. Jesus gives the sinner the kiss of peace
12. Joy in the soul and joy in heaven at the return of a sinner

Other Activities:

a) Children will find stories of conversion in readers; e.g., St. Peter, St. Mary Magdalen.

b) Study the poems, "Speak, Little Voice," Rev. Earls, S.J.; "Come to Jesus," Father Faber; "Discontent," Sarah Jewett; "The Very Time," M. D. Thayer.

c) Instruction on reverence and gratitude to parents. Definite situations and problems should be discussed.

d) Continue booklet on the Parables.

Pupil's Readings:

Rosary Reader, "The Prodigal Son," page 122.

Our Sacraments, Father Kelly, "The Merciful Father," page 26.

Teacher's References:

The Holy Bible, Luke, xv. 11–32, "The Prodigal Son."

The Little Ones, "Confession," page 122.

Practical Aids, "Conscience," pages 76–80.

Journeys of Jesus, Vol. II, "The Prodigal Son," Chapter XXI.

Jesus of Nazareth, pages 281–84.

Public Life, Bishop Goodier, Chapters 25 and 27.

During the instruction on Confession stress these questions:

What is Contrition?

What is Confession?

What sins are we bound to confess?

What should we do, if we cannot remember the number of our sins?

What is the Sacrament of Penance?

What must we do to receive the sacrament worthily?

What would we do before beginning the examination of conscience?

Teacher's Notes:

Review of the Parables

Arrange children into groups for a socialized recitation. With the help of the pictures, let them tell the stories to each other. Have them select their own chairmen.

They may also relate the stories and describe the pictures to other classes in the school; or give the dramatizations of them.

UNIT VII

SOME BEAUTIFUL WORDS OF JESUS

Jesus Blesses Little Children
March 1st Week

Introduction:

Start this Unit by telling the children that Jesus loved to be with little children; that the beautiful words He spoke when He was living were also meant for all of us living today. Study the picture which introduces this Unit. Make very vivid to the children that Jesus is whispering to each one of them as He is doing to the child on the picture. Let them suggest the conversation that is being held by Jesus and the child.

Presentation:

Write these questions on the board or give each child a mimeographed set before reading the lesson. Direct them to find the answers to the questions while they are reading silently:

1. When did this beautiful story happen?
2. Why did the mothers bring their children to Jesus?
3. Why was Jesus tired?
4. What did the Apostles say to the mothers?
5. Did Jesus like what the Apostles said to the mothers?
6. What did He tell them?
7. What did He mean by the words *suffer* and *kingdom of heaven?*
8. What did the happy children do?
9. What did Jesus do to them?
10. What does Jesus say to you?

Have the children, arranged in groups, ask each other these

questions. After this they may select the best reader in their group to read the lesson aloud, while they listen.

Let each one answer the exercise at the end of the lesson, page 118.

Jesus and a Rich Young Man
March 2nd Week

Introduction:

Review Questions: What were the beautiful words Jesus said about the children? What were the words He said to the children? What are the words of the Lord Jesus to you, His little child?

Presentation:

In the new lesson for today, Jesus and a Rich Young Man, we hear Jesus saying more beautiful words. He said them not only to the young man, but He said them for all of us, too. The young man asked Jesus a very important question: "Good Master, what must I do to reach heaven?"

Let the children suggest what to do to reach heaven. Now study the picture, *Christ and the Rich Young Man,* by Hofmann, and the picture in the text. Call attention to the love in Jesus' Holy Face, to the poor whom Jesus is showing the rich man. Now ask the children again what they think Jesus is asking the young man to do? After their discussion read the story to them. Tell them to watch for the holy words of Jesus to him and to them. Speak very simply and beautifully of the priesthood and sisterhood. It may be that a vocation may result in later years by just a few simple words spoken to children even at this early age. When the lesson has been read a number of times, return to the picture and let them retell the story. Suggest to them to take their book home and to read the story to their parents.

End the lesson with the exercise, "Something to Write," page 108.

A Miracle and a Promise
March 2nd Week

Introduction:

Review Questions: What were the beautiful words Jesus said about little children? What did He say to the rich young man? What may Jesus say to you some day? Would you like to follow Him?

Presentation:

Our lesson today is about a grand miracle and a grand promise of Jesus. One day Jesus and His Apostles went up into the mountain. Thousands of people followed Him. He loved them all. He looked into their hearts and He knew that they loved Him, too.

Continue telling the story so far as to arouse the enthusiasm of the children. Make very vivid the march of the people up the mountain, the kindness of the Lord Jesus, going in and out among them, laying His holy hands upon them and healing them. Describe the hunger of the people and the sympathy of Jesus for them. Stress the fact that there were thousands of people with the Lord.

"Now read the story quietly. When you have found out how the hungry people received enough to eat, you may stand."

Let them read quietly. Pass from one child to the next, encouraging, suggesting, helping where it is necessary in the reading.

When the children know what has happened in the story up to the miracle, let them tell it. Then have them finish the story and tell about the twelve baskets full left over.

"After the people had seen the miracle, their shouts rang over the mountains and valleys: 'This is the King of the Jews!' The Apostles were filled with joy for now their Jesus would be crowned King. But Jesus did not wish it. In sweet but firm tones, He told the people to return home. Soon all were gone, and Jesus and His Apostles were alone!

"Tomorrow we will read about the grand promise that Jesus made."

Introduction:

With the aid of a picture of the Multiplication of the Loaves and Fishes, let the children repeat the story of the grand miracle.

Presentation:

Surely now the people knew that Jesus is God. Soon the people were again with Jesus. This time instead of giving them something to eat, He gave them a grand promise. Sister will read about it in your book on page 121. Who will be able to tell what the promise is?

Read the story a number of times and let the children tell what the great promise is. Explain it carefully to them. Study the picture of the Last Supper, and tell them briefly that this was the fulfillment of the Blessed Sacrament, which will be studied later.

Continue the booklet on the miracles; also the Doctrine Booklet. Write short sentences in these books, illustrating them with original drawings or with pictures.

The children may read the stories suggested under "Pupil's Readings" during the library period and repeat them to the others who have not read them.

Have a final oral reading of the two parts of the story.

Teacher's References:

The Holy Bible, Matthew, Chapter XIV.

Practical Aids, "Prayers at Meals," page 80; "Obedience," page 38; "Spiritual Communion," page 80; "The Last Supper," page 114.

The Little Ones, "Teacher Tells a Story," Vol. I, page 88; "The Omnipotence of God," page 88.

Jesus of Nazareth, Chapters 22 and 29.

The Public Life, Bishop Goodier, Chapter 32, "Jesus and the Children"; Bishop Goodier, Chapter 33, "The Rich Young Man"; Bishop Goodier, Chapter 36, "The Question of the Chief Commandment."

Jesus' Own Prayer
March 3rd Week

Introduction:

Show the children a picture of *Christ at Prayer*. Study it carefully with them. Have other pictures of people at prayer mounted and placed about the classroom. The children can be encouraged to find such pictures and to mount them.

Presentation:

"Sister will read the story of the grandest prayer in the world. You will find it on page 127 of your books." The teacher will read it very slowly and with great devotion.

Study the practical lessons for each petition, as suggested in the following:

Our Father. God is the Father of all of us. He created us. We are His very own children. God is the Father of everyone on earth, Chinese, Japanese, Indians, Negroes. We are all sisters and brothers in God's big family.

Who art in heaven. Heaven is so beautiful that no one can describe it. It is God's special home. He wants us all to come to heaven with Him. Only good people will go to heaven. (Chisholm, "Our Father who art in Heaven," pages 74–108.)

Hallowed be Thy Name. The name of God is the holiest word that can be said. Whenever we say the name of God, of Jesus, devoutly, we adore Him. We must praise the name of God and only say it in prayer and in holy talk. That is what the word *hallowed* means. Praised, honored, loved be the name of God. (Chisholm, "Hallowed be Thy Name," pages 109–145.)

Thy Kingdom come. God is the great powerful King who made heaven and earth, who made all men and angels. We must adore our King so that one day He will take us to heaven. Every man's heart should be pure and holy because it belongs to God. That is God's kingdom on earth. Now not all men let God live in their hearts, they let the devil live in them. They commit sin and so drive their King, God, out of their hearts.

When they die, God cannot take those bad people into His Kingdom, heaven. When we say, "Thy Kingdom come," we pray that God will pardon these bad people; that He will live again in their hearts and take them with Him to heaven. (Chisholm, "Thy Kingdom Come," pages 146–180.)

Thy Will be done on earth as it is in heaven. To do the Will of God is always to do what is right and to accept anything He sends us, joy, sorrow, pain or pleasure, sickness, health, death. We ask God to help us and everybody else on earth to do His holy will. Only if we do what God wants us to do, will we reach heaven. In heaven, everybody is happy to obey God all the time. (Chisholm, "Thy Will be Done," page 81.)

Give us this day our daily bread. When we say these words, we ask our good Father in heaven to give us all that we need to live and to remain good. We ask for all our food, not for bread only. Then, too, we ask God for Holy Communion, the food of our soul. (Chisholm, "Give us this Day," pages 217–254.)

Forgive us our trespasses. Trespasses is just a big word for sin. We mean forgive us our sins. We are asking God's pardon, making an act of sorrow, for the many, many sins we have committed.

As we forgive those who trespass against us. At times our playmates offend us. We must forgive them and not be angry at them. We must forgive them even if they have not been sorry. God will only forgive us our sins, if we forgive the wrong others have done us. (Chisholm, pages 255–289.)

Lead us not into temptation. We should always do what is right. Sometimes we would like to do what is naughty. A big red apple is on another boy's desk. The devil says to you, "Take it, nobody will see you." A little voice in you says, "No, don't take it. It is not yours. You will offend God." The devil is *tempting* you to do wrong. When we say, "Lead us not into temptation," we are praying to God always to help us do the right thing, no matter how hard the *temptation* is. (Chisholm, pages 290–325.)

But deliver us from evil. These words mean that we ask God to free us from anything that could harm us in our soul or in our body. The greatest evil and the only one that can harm our soul is sin.

Evils that harm the body are sickness, fire, robbers. We ask our good Father in heaven to free us from all evils of body and soul, so we can serve Him better. (Chisholm, pages 326–360.)

During the English classes of the day's study discuss these poems: "A Child's Evening Prayer," Coleridge; "Different Ways," Thayer; "A Prayer to Mary," Father Hughes; "Thought," Thayer.

During a library period let the children read these stories: *New Catholic Reader,* "The Lord's Prayer"; *Cathedral,* "A Prayer," page 70; *Ideal,* II, "The Creator"; *American,* II, "A Little Boy's Prayer," page 1.

Explain these questions to the children, taken from the *Baltimore Catechism,* on prayer.

What is prayer? Explain that we pray to adore God, to thank Him, to ask for His help, to ask Him to forgive us.

When should we pray? Review the morning, evening, and meal prayers.

End the lesson with a final reading of the story and the exercise, "Ask Yourself," page 128.

Teacher's References:

The Little Ones, "The Our Father," pages 62–67.

Teacher Tells a Story, "The Lord's Prayer," pages 46–75.

The Catechism in Examples, "The Our Father," pages 74–358.

Teacher's Handbook to the Catechism, "The Lord's Prayer," pages 186–198; 252–256.

Teacher's Notes:

Jesus Speaks to Me
March 3rd Week

Introduction:

Study once more the picture introducing the Unit. Tell the children to imagine they are the children in the picture and Jesus is speaking these words just to them.

Presentation:

While the children are looking at the picture, the teacher will read very slowly and softly the words of the lesson. Repeat the reading as often as the children wish to hear it. Incidentally they will thus learn the Scripture texts.

After this reading, discuss with the children the meaning of each sentence. Let them talk freely and informally, telling any stories of their own experience or any which they may have read.

A coöperative booklet could be made by having the children cut out, in colored letters, the sentences of the text, making a poster of each. These may be placed in the school corridors for a number of days.

End this Unit with a general reading party. As suggested before, the children will arrange the program, select their various committees for reading definite parts aloud, for writing invitations, for decorating, for reciting poems. All this will be very informal and will serve as an excellent review of the Unit.

UNIT VIII
THE SADDEST STORY EVER TOLD
Lenten Season

At the beginning of the Lenten Season, explain very simply the purpose of the season, how even little children can show their love for Jesus by doing small acts of mortification. Suggest *one* comparatively big penance they can do all during Lent; e.g.:

I will go to Holy Mass every morning during Lent when I can.

I will not go to the movies during Lent.

I will go to Confession often (once a week) during Lent.

Little daily practices should not be neglected.

Ash Wednesday. A short instruction on the devotions of the day should not be omitted. Have the children understand and memorize the words said to Adam: "Dust thou art and unto dust shalt thou return." Make very sacred in the young child's mind the *Sacramentals* of the Church.

Stations of the Cross. Spend much of the Lenten Season instructing the children on the passion of Jesus. Study on an average two stations a week. Teach the children the simple prayers for each station. A booklet by a Religious of the Cenacle, entitled *Stations of the Cross for Children* (5 cents), is very fitting for children of the second grade; also *The Stations in Poetry,* by M. D. Thayer.

Set the stations, as they are being studied, in the sand table.

Use a set of Station Cards or art pictures suggested in the following paragraph for this. The figures also to be cut out of art pictures, supported with cardboard backs, and arranged to illustrate the respective station studied. If the table is large enough, have the entire Way of the Cross, with each station in its proper setting and placed there just as it is being studied.

Pictures for Study:

Leaving the Praetorium, Doré; *Christ Falls Under His Cross,* Thiersch; *Christ Meets His Mother,* Raphael; *Veronica,* Hofmann; *The Holy Woman,* Deluge; *Golgatha,* Clement; *Nailing to the Cross,* Hole; *The Crucifixion,* Munkácsy; *The Night of the Crucifixion,* Doré; *Christ Between Two Thieves,* Rubens; *The Descent From the Cross,* Rubens; *The Sorrowful Mother,* J. Wagenfrenner; *The Entombment,* Hofmann; *In the Tomb,* Hofmann; *Return From Calvary,* Schonaltz; *Christ the King.*

After the Stations are quite well known, take the class to church and there have them study and pray the stations, the teacher leading from one station to the other and saying the prayers aloud, while the children go with her.

A booklet, edited by a Religious of the Cenacle, published by the Paulist Press, 401 West 59 St., New York, entitled, *A Thought a Day for Lent for Children,* gives a beautiful preparation for each day of Lent, a simple resolution and an ejaculation for the day. The price is only five cents. Each teacher ought to have one and use it every day of Lent with her class. Have each child make one of his own.

Penance Booklet:

At the beginning of Lent, a booklet can be started referring to the season. The cover of purple color to signify penance, a cross cut from white paper can be pasted on it; also a picture of the Crucifixion. On the inside sheets the children can write the resolutions for each day and the ejaculation they wish to say often during the day. Most prominent should be their "BIG" penance. Let the children be free to make this booklet as they wish.

At the close of Lent, the large school crucifix can be arranged in a setting of ferns and flowers in the front of the classroom. The children will place their booklets on the table.

Holy Week

To the Teacher:

Let the work of this holy time be a fitting preparation for both yourself and the pupils for the Feast of Easter. The instruction shall consist each day in a holy, loving, inspiring study of the liturgy of the week. Do not expect little children to remember many details. Of utmost importance is the instilling into their hearts, according to their capacity, a love for the Savior, a horror for sin, a desire to live a holy life. Encourage those who have already received Holy Communion to fulfill their Easter duty on the great Feast of the Blessed Sacrament, Holy Thursday.

Introduction:

Let each day's lesson start with a hymn to Jesus. Poems that they know can also be said as prayers.

Presentation:

Monday. Review the entry into Jerusalem and the Palm Sunday ceremonies; tell the children why the statues are veiled.

Tuesday. Review the Last Supper and explain to the children the Holy Thursday adoration. Speak of the love of Jesus in the Blessed Sacrament for men, but in particular for His own child; of the longing of the Heart of Jesus for us all.

Wednesday. Review briefly the passion, dwelling entirely on the love of Jesus for us all, how through His death heaven is now ours. Describe quite briefly the striking ceremonies of Good Friday and Holy Saturday.

Thursday. (If school is in session, discuss the following points. If school is not in session, these ought to be taken on Wednesday in a special Religion Period.) The Resurrection, the greatest miracle ever performed, the greatest proof that Jesus is God. Explain the significance of Easter Day.

Teacher's References:

The Holy Bible, "The Passion and Death of Our Lord."

The Visible Church, Rev. Sullivan, Lesson 49.

Holy Week Ceremonies.

Practical Aids, "The Passion of Christ," pages 120–124; "Sand-Table Project on the Passion," page 232; "To Teach the Children the Passion," page 264.

The Little Ones, "Calvary," page 110.

Journeys With Jesus, Vol. III, Chapters XVIII, XIX, and XX.

Wonder Stories of God's People, page 276.

Jesus of Nazareth, "The Seven Last Words," pages 354–369.

Teacher Tells a Story, Vol. II, "The Death and Burial," page 142.

Teacher's Notes:

The Saddest Story Ever Told
Introductory Lesson
April 1st Week

Introduction:

Begin the study of the passion with questions: Why did Jesus come to this earth? (Lead the children to the idea of the Redemption.) Who committed the first sin? What kind of sin was it? Who can tell the story of Adam and Eve? How did God punish them? Whom did God promise to send to this earth to save them? What sin did we inherit from our first parents? Did Jesus have to redeem us, too? Could anybody else besides Jesus have redeemed us and opened the gates of heaven?

Presentation:

Speak to the children in simple language about the *love* of Jesus for all men, particularly for each one of us; how He showed this love by coming down to earth to teach us the way to heaven; how He was ready now after thirty-three years on earth, to die on the cross in order to open heaven for us.

Describe briefly the Paschal Feast of the Jews; how each good Jew went to Jerusalem to celebrate the feast; that Jesus and His disciples were also on their journey to the Holy City. Make the application here of the Sunday obligation of hearing Mass.

Tell about the enemies of Jesus who were waiting for an opportunity to put Him to death; that it was only because of His own will that Jesus was going to die. Stress again the *love* of Jesus. How can a good child show his love toward Jesus?

Close this introductory lesson with the Acts of Faith, Hope, and Charity said slowly by the class, and with a hymn the children would like to sing.

Hosanna!

Introduction:

Start this lesson with a study of the picture, *The Triumphal Entry,* by Deger; the picture in the child's text. Call attention to the majestic appearance of Christ the King, to the intense enthusiasm of the people, and to the joy on the faces of the Apostles. Tell the beginning of the story including the following points: Christ's stay at Bethany the previous night; the order He gave to the Apostles in the morning; the story of the man with the colt; the multitude following from Bethany and those coming from the city to meet Jesus.

Presentation:

Children, in your readers you will find the story about Jesus, the great King. Read it quietly now.

After sufficient time for the silent reading, ask the children to repeat the story. Aid them with questions.

"Who will read the part which tells what the children sang? The men and women?" Explain that these words, Hosanna, etc., are said every day at Mass, just before Jesus comes down upon the altar. Have the children memorize the words of the

Sanctus and Benedictus and encourage them to repeat these during Mass.

"Read the part which tells what the people did to show their love for Jesus. What did the children do?"

Make a good and brief comparison of Jesus entering in triumph into Jerusalem and the beautiful processions of the Church in honor of the Blessed Sacrament. Stress the honor for little boys and girls, who, like the Jewish children, walk and strew flowers before the dear Jesus. Repeat this instruction every time before a procession.

"Read how Jesus spent the day in Jerusalem."

"Who would like to read the entire story for the class?" Have the child step before the class to do this.

Dramatize the story. Divide the children into two groups, one staying in the classroom, while the other goes into the corridor. Those in the corridor represent the people coming out of Jerusalem to meet Jesus. Those in the classroom are the Apostles, Martha, Mary, Lazarus, and the other friends from Bethany. No representation of Jesus is necessary. Groups carry twigs of trees, flowers, spread their garments, and sing hymns of joy. Let the children walk about the classroom a number of times. For further information, see Educational Series, Dr. Shields, *Religion Book III,* page 108.

Discuss the blessing and the use of palms.

Creative Art and Writing Song: Let the children cut out in silhouette the figures of Christ on the donkey, of children waving palms. Even though the work is not perfect, place the various contributions about the classroom during the study of the lesson.

Have the children write a conversation which they think Jesus held with the children in the procession.

Let the children create a song of joy and praise.

Continue the Penance Booklet; encourage the children to make it as beautiful as possible for the love of Jesus. Again see *Art Education Through Religion,* Penance Booklet, Vol. II, page 32.

Complete this lesson with the exercise, "Something to Do," page 132. The children will select one of the suggested activities. If they have selected paper cutting, exhibit their work; also the story which they have written may be read during the Oral English class. If a song is composed, praise the child or group for its efforts and let it sing its work for the class.

The Temple of God
April 1st Week

Introduction:

Have the children repeat briefly the story of the victorious entry into Jerusalem. Sing a hymn in honor of Jesus.

Presentation:

Tell the children as much of the day's story as will arouse their interest. Among the points are the following: the custom of offering animals, especially lambs, at the Paschal Season; the din and confusion of men and animals before the holy temple of God; the arrival of Jesus from Bethany with His Apostles. Make the presentation very vivid.

"Jesus looked upon this scene before the house of His Father with deep sorrow. Suddenly everybody turned toward Jesus. He had said something. Read it. When you know what Jesus said, you may stand."

Let them read the story quietly to the words of Jesus. "What do you think Jesus did? Now finish the story and tell what happened."

"Who can tell me what happened?" Let them tell the story. Show them the picture, *Driving the Sellers out of the Temple,* by Hofmann. Have them note the expressions on the different faces—majesty and power in the face of Jesus; fear in the faces of the buyers and sellers; awe in those of the Apostles.

"Who would like to step before the class with his book, and ask the other children questions on the lesson?" Have them ask each other until the story is well known.

Work the exercise, "Something to Do," page 134. Take each question carefully and let the children answer them orally.

End the lesson by telling them the story of this day; Jesus had watched the people throwing money into the coffers just to be seen by others. A poor widow threw in her last penny for love of God. Speak of her reward in the praise of Jesus. Show the picture, *The Widow's Mite*, by Meith. The children should be encouraged also to give their mite at the Sunday collections. Jesus will reward them for this sacrifice. If they have but little, Jesus will be pleased with the little. If they have much, they should give much to the Lord.

Teacher's References:

The Holy Bible, Matthew, xxi. 1–12; Mark, ii. 1–11; Luke, xix. 28–48; John, xii. 1–20.

Bishop Goodier, Chapters 35 and 36.

The Little Ones, "Entry Into Jerusalem," page 134.

Wonder Stories of God's People, "Hosanna," page 268.

Jesus of Nazareth, "Jerusalem!" Chapter XXXVII (very attractive).

Teacher's Notes:

Judas the Thief
April 1st Week

Introduction:

Tell the story of the growing hatred of the Pharisees and the High Priests toward Jesus; of their jealousy and their plans to kill Jesus; of Jesus' own Will to die for the sins of the world.

Presentation:

One of the Apostles of Jesus had become a very, very wicked man, a thief. It was Judas. How often Jesus had warned Judas, but alas! Judas would not listen to the sweet words of Jesus. He had become a secret enemy of his loving Master.

One day, shortly after the triumphal entry of Jesus into Jerusalem, Judas did a terrible thing. Would you like to know about it? On page 134, in your religion book, you can see what Judas did.

Let the children read the story. When they have finished it, study the picture, *The Temptation of Judas*, by Prell. Let them tell the story over and over again in connection with the picture study.

Stress that it was the one evil passion which Judas did not try to conquer that caused this awful sin. It finally drove him to commit the most horrible crime the world had ever seen. Perhaps from his childhood Judas had been stealing.

Give a thorough instruction on honesty, the necessity of returning anything that we have ever stolen, or of paying for it. Take a good review of the seventh commandment. See *Teaching the Ten Commandments* for practical problems, pages 149–170.

"Open your books to page 135. This story tells us more about Judas. Sister will read it for you. See whether you can answer these questions: To whom did Jesus give the bread? Why did Jesus give the bread to him?"

Read the story with much expression to the children and have the children read it aloud a few times.

End the lesson with an Act of Contrition in reparation for Judas' terrible sin. Also say the prayers at the end of the lesson.

The Grandest Gift of Jesus
April 2nd Week

To the Teacher:

This story with all its parts belongs to the work on the passion chronologically. Explain this to the children and tell them that the passion stories will be continued later.

Introduction:

Sing a hymn to the Blessed Sacrament. Review Questions: Why had Jesus come to earth? Why did the Pharisees wish to kill Him? Who was the traitor? What did Judas do? Did Jesus know about the terrible plot to kill Him? Could He have saved Himself? Why did He not do so? Why did Jesus want to die? Remember, it needed only a word of God to create us; but it needed the *Blood* of Jesus to redeem us.

Presentation:

Tell the various parts of the story of this Holy Thursday. Expand the following, however, not too much in detail:

a) The last night with His friends and surely with His Mother in Bethany.

b) Peter and John sent ahead to prepare the supper chamber for the Paschal Supper. (Let the children dramatize this.)

c) The preparation for the supper. Peter buys the lamb without a spot or blemish; the cakes of unleavened bread, the wine and the water; the arrangement of the table, the beauty of the Upper Room, where the most wonderful thing was going to happen.

d) The departure of Jesus from Bethany; probably Mother Mary and His friends went along to serve Jesus and the Apostles.

"Now let us turn to our books. We shall read first of all the story of Jesus and Judas at the Last Supper."

The teacher will read the story, slowly, beautifully, while the children follow it in their books. Read only Part I.

Study the picture, *The Last Supper,* by Da Vinci. It is this very moment which the artist has portrayed. Mark the various expressions, especially those of Jesus, John, Peter, and Judas. Let the children repeat the story while they study the picture. Do not fear to spend too much time in this picture study. If properly presented, it will make a lifelong impression on the hearts of the children.

"Let us continue the story." The teacher will read in a very beautiful, impressive way. Study the picture, *The Washing of the Feet,* in the children's text. Again let them look at it and talk about it as long as they wish. Have them retell the story of Peter. Encourage them to memorize the exact quotations and to tell these stories to their parents in the words of Holy Scripture.

"Now we come to the most wonderful story in your book." The teacher will read in a most reverent way the story of the Holy Eucharist. After this reading let the children spend as much time as they wish in reading the stories quietly and in looking at the pictures of their text and any other art pictures. These latter, in as large numbers as possible about the Holy Eucharist, the Last Supper, the Mass, should be mounted and kept before the eyes of the children throughout the study of this lesson. At times ask individual children to get the picture they like best and to tell the story connected with it to the class.

Have them memorize the words of Consecration. Encourage them to say: "My Lord and my God," at the elevation of the Host during Mass; and "My Jesus, mercy," at the elevation of the Chalice. Review an instruction on the Mass. Tell the children that the first Mass was said by Jesus Himself on this very night of the Last Supper; that the Mass and the Sacrifice of the cross are the one and the same. Ask them questions and explain them on the Mass:

a) Ask when and where are the bread and wine changed into the Body and Blood of Christ.

b) What is the Mass?

c) Is the Mass the same Sacrifice as that of the Cross?

d) Is it a mortal sin not to hear Mass on Sunday or on a holyday of obligation? (Explain these days.)

e) What is the Holy Eucharist?

f) When did Christ institute the Holy Eucharist?

g) What is Holy Communion?

h) What is necessary to make a good Communion?

Speak about the reverence before the Blessed Sacrament, proper genuflections, tipping the hat while passing the church, making visits to Jesus.

Tell the children that on this evening when Jesus said: "Do this for a commemoration of Me," He made the Apostles His first *priests*. Instill a great respect in the hearts of the children for the priests.

Teach the children proper manners and the proper way of addressing the priest.

Above all encourage them to pray often for the priests throughout the world, including the pope and bishops.

Other Activities:

a) Creative Art: "Children, cut out a host and a chalice to paste into your Doctrine Booklet." See *Art Education*, Vol. II, page 35. Write the words of Christ beneath the pictures.

b) Creative Music: Have the children write the words and music of a song to Jesus in the Blessed Sacrament, according to the method previously described.

c) Study the following poems: "Blessed Candle," Joseph Collins; "Communion," C. Giltinan; "After a Visit to the Blessed Sacrament," S. M. St. John.

d) During silent reading periods let the children find stories about the Blessed Sacrament in various readers. They may tell these to the class. Stories about Blessed Imelda, St. Pancratius, Little Nellie, St. Stanislaus, are very suitable.

Have the children read aloud the parts of The Grandest Gift of Jesus in class, and then work the exercise, "Something to Do," page 141.

End the entire work with a visit to Jesus in the Blessed Sacrament as an act of thanksgiving for the Eucharist. Make this visit as a class.

Pupil's Readings:

Ideal Second, "A Child's Wish," page 91.

American Cardinal, "Blessed Imelda," page 140; "St. Cyril," page 118.

American Second, "A Lover of Children," page 112.

Marywood, "Blessed Imelda," page 187; "Finding You," page 196.

Life of Our Blessed Lord, "The Last Supper," pages 58–61.

Our Sacraments, "Bread From Heaven," pages 46–63; "The Priesthood."

The Catholic Child, "The Wonderful Gift," page 128.

My Gift to Jesus, by Sister of St. Dominic.

My Mass Book, by Sister Servants of the I. H. M.

Teacher's References:

The Holy Bible.

Jesus of Nazareth, "The Night in Which He Was Betrayed," pages 322–344.

Journeys of Jesus, Vol. III, Chapter VIII, "Judas Sells Jesus"; Chapter XII, "On the Way to the Garden."

Practical Aids, Section V, "The Blessed Sacrament."

The Little Ones, "The Blessed Sacrament," page 76; "The Last Supper," page 135; "The Real Presence," page 137; "The Holy Mass," page 138; "Holy Communion," page 139; "How to Hear Holy Mass," page 146.

The Saddest Story Ever Told
Mt. Olivet
April 3rd Week

Introduction:

Review Questions: How did Jesus show His special love for us at the Last Supper? How did our Lord give us Himself? What holy words did He use? Who said the first Mass? Who were the first priests? What did Jesus tell the Apostles to do in memory of Him? What happens in the Mass every morning? Why is Jesus in the Holy Eucharist? How long will He stay in the Blessed Sacrament?

Let us sing a hymn to Jesus. (O Sacrament Most Holy.)

Presentation:

After the wonderful Last Supper, Jesus, the Savior of the world, was ready to redeem the world. He and His Apostles walked out of the city to a place in which He loved to pray, the Mount of Olives.

Continue the story only so far as to arouse the interest of the class. Then let them read Parts VI and VII and retell the story. Explain what Jesus meant; how He tried to keep Peter from doing something very wrong, as He had tried to keep Judas. Peter, too, was very proud.

Describe the Garden of Gethsemane, where Jesus had always loved to pray. Show the picture *In Gethsemane,* by Hofmann. Tell the story with feeling and reverence. Explain the words, *Rabbi, betray, redemption.*

Describe the prayer of Jesus in as many details as the children are capable of understanding. Stress the prayer: "Father, not My Will, but Thine be done."

"Now let us read the story in our religion books. Read it quietly and then tell us about the traitor and about the dear Jesus." Let them read the story. While they are doing so, pass from one to the other, asking a question about any part of the story.

Show them pictures of any of the scenes their story relates, e.g., *The Sleep of the Disciples,* by Hofmann, Bida; *The Kiss of Judas,* Geiger. Mount all the pictures that you can possibly get on the passion and keep these before their eyes throughout the study. Teach them the first Sorrowful Mystery of the Rosary.

"Let us read the story aloud. Who will read all the explaining parts? Who will read the parts Jesus spoke? Peter's words?" End this reading with an Act of Contrition.

During the course of the day, let the children arrange the sand table to illustrate the road or path leading from the city, the Brook Cedron, the Mount of Olives with the Garden of Gethsemane.

Jesus Before the High Priest
April 3rd Week

Introduction:

Review Questions: What did Jesus think and pray about in the garden for three hours? How great was His grief and sorrow? What were the Apostles doing? Who came and consoled Jesus? Who was the traitor? How did he betray Jesus? What did Jesus say to him? Why did Jesus let Himself be bound and taken prisoner? What had Jesus begun?

Presentation:

Tell the children only so much of the story as will arouse their curiosity. Let them read the story quietly until they can find the answer to the question, What did Jesus mean when He said to the high priest: "I am!"

"Read what happened to Jesus when He said: 'I am!'

"Read what Jesus did when the soldiers were so cruel to Him.

"Read how Jesus spent the whole night." Explain to them how Jesus was in the power of the enemy all that night.

Discuss with them daily situations in which they can practice patience for the love of Jesus. Stress the point that they must always tell the truth, no matter what the result may be. For Practical Problems, see *Teaching the Ten Commandments*—the fifth and eighth commandments.

Draw the attention of the children's minds to the love we show Jesus when we suffer willingly for Him; how nights of pain can be offered to Jesus in remembrance of this last night of His on earth.

End the lesson with one oral reading and with an Act of Love and Contrition.

Peter Denies Christ
April 3rd Week

Introduction:

Have the children turn to the lesson Jesus Washes the Feet of His Apostles. Let them read aloud the story of Jesus and Peter. Then read aloud the story On the Way to the Mount of Olives. Let them tell the two stories about Peter. Finally draw attention to the fact that the Apostles and Peter in particular left Jesus alone in the hands of His enemies.

Presentation:

Show the picture of Peter. Tell the children just a part of the story and let them read the rest from their own books. Have them read only to the first denial of Peter. When they have reached this part let them tell it.

"Do you think Peter denied Jesus again? Read the next few lines and see what Peter did." Let them tell it when they know what had happened. "What do you think Peter did then? Your story will tell you." Let them answer the question again. "How many times did Peter deny Jesus? Why do you think Peter denied His dear Lord? After this third time something wonderful happened to Peter. The next part of the story tells you. Read it quietly and tell me what Peter finally did."

Now study the picture in the text or any other picture of the repentance of Peter. The children will tell what the picture now means to them. Add the beautiful little details you like.

Give a brief instruction on the Act of Perfect Contrition. Review the prayer with the class and encourage them to make this act every night before going to sleep and always after having been naughty.

Read the lesson aloud once more. Let one child take all the explanatory part, while others will read the conversational parts. Always have them stand before the class while giving this longer reading.

Jesus Before Pilate
April 4th Week

Introduction:

Let the children repeat briefly the events in the passion from Mt. Olivet to the repentance of Peter.

Presentation:

With the aid of the picture in the text and also any art pictures showing Christ before Pilate, tell the story to the class. Teach them to pray the First Station of the Cross.

After this informal work, read the lesson to the children as far as the scourging. Study a picture of the scourging, but do not go too much into detail.

Continue reading the story about the crowning with thorns to the children. Study a picture of the thorn-crowned Savior. While so doing, encourage the children always to keep their minds filled with good and beautiful thoughts for love of Jesus crowned with thorns.

Finish the reading of the story to the children about the sentence of Pilate. Have the pictures, *Ecce Homo*, by Schaefer, *Christ Before Pilate*, by Munkácsy, ready for a picture study at this point. Let the children ponder upon both the stories and the pictures as long as they wish. Often during the day let them walk about the room, examining any of the pictures on the passion displayed about the room.

Teach the second and third mysteries of the Sorrowful Rosary.

End this lesson by letting three children read the three big parts of the story, and work the exercise on page 151.

A study of the Stations should be correlated with these reading lessons. See the Introduction to this Unit for this study.

Jesus on the Cross
April 4th Week

(To the Teacher: In preparation for this short lesson, arrange the large classroom crucifix in a beautiful setting of ferns and flowers on a table in the front or corner of the room. Place vigil lights about it. Have a *prie-dieu* before the shrine.)

Introduction:

Explain to the children that for today's religion lesson, each child may take his book, kneel on the *prie-dieu* and read the little poem aloud to his Jesus on the cross. Then he may place his Penance Booklet at the feet of Jesus. While the children are reading, let the others be arranged in groups and quietly be busy at the sand table, putting up the Stations; finding poems in other books about Jesus or stories about the passion; clay modeling or drawing crosses, spears, nails, the Hill of Calvary; or telling each other the stories of the passion.

Teach the fourth and fifth mysteries of the Sorrowful Rosary.
Presentation:
Each child will read the poem as explained above.

The poem "Nails," by Father Feeney, S.J., may be written on the board and explained during the Oral Expression class.

Jesus Savior of the World
April 4th Week

Introduction:
Teach the children the hymn, "The Cross So Tall," by Father Tabb. For the music and words see *Practical Aids,* page 250. Have the children repeat the poems "Jesus on the Cross" and "Nails."

Presentation:
Speak to the children a few minutes on the *love* of Jesus for all men, but especially for each one of them; how Jesus thought of each one; how He was keeping the *grand promise of God to men,* which God gave to Adam and Eve in the Garden of Paradise; how by His death heaven was again opened to all good men. Let them kneel down and say a prayer of thanksgiving to Jesus on the cross.

During the three long hours on the cross, Jesus spoke such loving, tender words. Your lesson on page 154 tells you some of these holy words of Jesus. Open your books and read until you know what the first words of Jesus are on the cross.

Explain the first word of Jesus carefully and make practical applications to the daily life of the children.

Talk to the children about the two robbers crucified with Jesus; how one was very wicked; but the other one, seeing that the Lord Jesus loved even His enemies, believed He was God.

"Jesus said a very beautiful sentence to one of the robbers. When you have found it in your books, you may tell the class."

Explain this second word to the children. Show a picture of this scene.

"Now there stood by the cross of Jesus, His Mother, and the disciple John, whom Jesus loved. They were the dearest, truest friends of Jesus on earth. Read the loving words Jesus spoke to them from the cross."

Give a short instruction on this word of Jesus, how from that moment Mary has been the mother of all men, and we have become her children. Study a picture of Mary and John at the cross of Jesus.

The next sentence tells you about a terrible suffering of Jesus. Read it and promise Jesus that you will often mortify (explain the word) yourself for love of Him.

Now read the last two words of Jesus on the cross. Explain to the children the meaning of these words.

Sister will finish reading the story of Christ's death for you.

Let the children read the story as often as they wish and read it again for them. With the help of these mounted pictures: *The Descent From the Cross*, by Rubens; *The Sorrowful Mother*, by J. Wagenbrenner; *The Entombment*, by Hofmann; *The Return From Calvary*, by Schonaltz, tell the stories.

Take these questions of the Catechism: What did Jesus suffer? On what day did He die? How did Jesus die? Why did He die?

Close the Unit by reading to the children the lesson "In Limbo" and explaining briefly.

The sand table can be arranged very beautifully to illustrate the hill of Calvary, the three empty crosses, the tomb a distance from Calvary.

Doctrine Booklet:

By this time the articles of the Creed about Jesus Christ up to the resurrection ought to be completed.

Final Review

Appoint one section of the Unit to each child in the class. Have him read or tell the story to the class. Let him use a picture illustrative of his story.

After this review let the children answer the questions in their text on page 157 orally.

Teacher's References:

The Holy Bible, all the Gospels on the Passion.

The Journeys of Jesus, Vol. III, Chapters XI, XII, XIII, XIV, XV, XVI.

Jesus of Nazareth, "The Suffering of Christ," pages 334–369; "The Seven Last Words," pages 354–369.

Practical Aids, "The Suffering and Death of Our Lord," pages 113–127; "Sand-Table Project on the Passion," page 232; "To Teach the Children the Passion," page 264.

The Little Ones, "Calvary," page 110.

Teacher's Notes:

UNIT IX
THE MOST GLORIOUS STORY EVER TOLD
The Resurrection

To the Teacher:

Let a most joyous spirit, the Easter spirit, pervade every instruction period. A song at the beginning of each will help much to create an atmosphere of joy and love. Any lovely hymn the children know to the Blessed Sacrament, to Mary, to St. Joseph, will be suitable.

As suggested in the Course, a Resurrection Booklet could be made. Cut out each page of the booklet in the shape of an Easter lily. Give the children a pattern for this. The cover sheet will be a lily cut out of good white drawing paper and colored to represent the petals of the flower. A small holy card representing Jesus Christ the Risen Savior should be pasted on this cover. Each of the other pages will contain a picture of the appearance, if possible, or any other illustration of any phase of the appearance, the name of the appearance in prominent letters, and the exact quotations together with any important event connected with the specific appearance. The following appearances are studied in the course. Names and quotations are suggestive for the booklet:

1. Jesus appeared to Mary His Holy Mother.

   (Any picture of the Virgin Mother is suitable.)

2. Jesus appeared to Mary Magdalen.

   Jesus saith to her, "MARY!"

   She saith to Him, "RABBONI!"

3. Jesus appeared in the Upper Room to the Apostles.

   Peace be to you!

Whose sins you shall forgive, they are forgiven them.
4. Jesus appeared to Thomas.

Bring hither thy hand and put it into My side.
My Lord and my God!

5. Jesus appeared on the seashore.

Cast your net on the right side of the ship.
It is the Lord!

6. Jesus appeared to Peter.

Simon, Son of John, lovest thou Me?
Lord, Thou knowest that I love Thee.
Feed My Lambs; feed My Sheep!

7. Jesus' Last Appearance.

Whilst He blessed them, He was carried up to heaven.
He sitteth at the right hand of God!

Part I. The First Easter Morning
May 1st Week

Introduction:

Sing an Easter hymn or "Holy God, We Praise Thy Name."
Review Questions: Why did Jesus die for us? Why were the
gates of heaven closed? What was done with the body of Jesus?
Where was the Soul of Jesus? Who else, do you think, was
there? (Mention especially Adam and Eve, Joachim, Anne, St.
John, St. Joseph.)

Presentation:

Jesus had promised that He would rise from the dead on the
third day. He had redeemed the world. His Soul was in Limbo,
bringing the good news of the Redemption to all the holy souls
there. It was early Sunday morning. Something grand happened!
Turn to your religion book to page 159. The story, "The First
Easter Morn," tells you about it. Read it quietly and see how
great the Lord Jesus is!

Let the children read the story quietly. After some minutes
ask the following:

"Read the part of the story which tells you where the Soul

of Jesus was." Stress the point that the souls were happy in Limbo, but were longing for heaven and God.

Read the part about the great miracle. What was the miracle? (Explain very simply that the Resurrection was the greatest proof that Jesus is God.) Who else came back from the dead? How did they come back? But how did Jesus come back from the dead? (Stress the difference between the Resurrection of Christ and the raising from the dead of the others by the word of Christ.)

"Read the part that tells how Jesus came out of the tomb." Explain very simply the power of Jesus' Body to pass from place to place even through walls.

"Read about the angel from heaven. What did he do? Can you tell how the angel looked?"

Speak to them of the resurrection of all men at the end of the world; how all the good will be saved, and the wicked will be punished in hell forever. Study the picture, *The Last Judgment,* by Michelangelo. Tell of the second coming of Christ as Judge in detail. Stress the truth that God Himself has revealed all this and His word must be the truth.

Explain these questions of the Catechism:

a) When will Christ judge us?

b) What is hell?

c) What is purgatory?

d) What is heaven?

Let the children illustrate parts of the story of the Resurrection in drawing, paper cutting, or on the sand table. The latter can be done by building the tomb in the side of the hill just as the sand-table project for Good Friday. The stone is lying before the tomb. An angel, cut from any art picture, can be put into the setting. The guards are prostrate before the tomb.

Teach the first Glorious Mystery of the Rosary.

Study any other art pictures: *Easter Morning,* by Hofmann; *He Is Risen,* by Plockhorst. Let the children repeat the story with the help of these pictures.

Suggest to them to bring the religious Easter cards which the family may receive, to school, to mount them and to help them with their booklet.

Doctrine Booklet:

Creed: On the third day He arose again from the dead.

Have one more oral reading of the Lesson on the Resurrection and finish it with the exercise, "Fill in the Spaces," page 160.

Part II. Appearance to Mary His Mother
May 1st Week

Introduction:

Sing a hymn to Mary. Ask the children to whom they think Jesus surely would have gone first. "Why do you think so? What was the Blessed Virgin Mary very likely doing while Jesus was in the grave? Did she know, do you think, that Jesus would rise from the dead?" Show them a picture of the Sorrowful Mother and let them tell why she is so sad.

Presentation:

Mary suffered much. But on this first Easter Day her dear Son Jesus turned all her sorrow into the greatest joy. Let us read the story about Jesus and His dear Mother on Easter Day. Who will read the story aloud for the rest of the class?

Select a very good reader, have him step before the class, and read it, while the others follow him in their books. (This child should have prepared the lesson well.)

Let them talk about the appearance. Tell the children that there were Seven Great Joys in the life of Mary. Let them make their suggestions which they might be. Talk about the following joys: the Annunciation, the Nativity, the Return from Egypt, the Finding of Christ. Another great joy of Mary's will be when she can take each one of us to the throne of God in heaven and say to Jesus: "My Son, this is my dear child, Henry, Mary. He loved me during his life on earth. Now, dear Jesus, bless him forever in heaven."

In honor of Mary, let the children give a short program, consisting of any poem, song, story they wish.

During the course of the day, the children will work the exercise at the end of their lesson, "Something to Do."

Part III. Mary Magdalen
May 1st Week

Introduction:

Sing a hymn to Jesus. Show the children the picture of *Mary Magdalen,* by Hofmann. Tell them the story of the intense grief of Mary. Study the picture and let the children repeat the story from the picture.

Presentation:

Would you like to read the story from your books? You will find it on page 162. While you are reading it, look at the picture, too.

Let them read and repeat the story to the class.

Read the part that tells how Mary Magdalen felt because Jesus was dead. Why did Mary love Jesus so much? (Tell the class that Mary had been a big sinner whom Jesus had so kindly forgiven. If you wish, tell here the story of her public penance in the house of Simon. Show the picture of her repentance.)

Speak of the love and forgiveness of Jesus toward children who are sorry for their sins and go to Confession. Stress Mary's Act of Contrition.

How did Mary find the tomb? Read what Mary did when she saw that the tomb was empty.

Read the part about the angels.

What did the Gardener say to Mary Magdalen? Read what she said to Him.

Read the part of the story which you like best.

Now let us read the entire story once more. Who will read all the parts that explain what is happening? Who will read Mary Magdalen's words? Who will read the Gardener's words? the angels? All step to the front of the class, and read it most beautifully for love of Jesus.

Dramatize: Mary at the empty tomb: Running back to Peter:

Peter and John and Mary returning to the tomb; their sorrow; the angel's words. Now let the children work at the Appearance Booklet. When this is finished have them work the exercise, "Something to Do," page 164. This exercise can also be worked during the course of day, correlating it with the composition work.

Part IV. On the Way to Emmaus
May 2nd Week

Introduction:

Tell the children of the sadness of some of the disciples of Jesus, who felt that Jesus was gone forever from them. On this same Easter day two of these disciples went from Jerusalem to Emmaus on business. While they were walking along the road, a Stranger joined them. It was the dear Lord Himself, but they did not know Him. Show them the picture, *To Emmaus,* by Hofmann, Plockhorst, and let them talk about it. In your story to them, tell the class about the conversation on the way.

Presentation:

When the two disciples drew near to the town, the Stranger acted as though He would go farther. They begged Him to stay with them as it was growing dark. We know who the Stranger is, but these disciples did not yet know. Would you like to read how they discovered it was their dear Jesus? You will find the story in your books.

Let the children read it quietly. Then show them the picture, *Supper at Emmaus,* by Titian, Muller, and have them repeat the beautiful story, as much in the words of the Scripture as possible.

Speak to the children on how they should often invite Jesus into their hearts in Holy Communion, if they have already received, or in Spiritual Communion. Jesus is always waiting for them in the tabernacle. It was the charity of the two disciples toward a stranger that brought them the wonderful grace of receiving the Holy Communion from the Master's own hands.

Jesus will receive as though it was done to Himself, all we do for others through love of Him. Let these little acts be a preparation to receive Jesus: "Jesus, this is for You. When You come into my heart the next time, please accept my little gifts." This "gift" can also be offered to Jesus when we visit Him in the Blessed Sacrament.

After another careful reading of the story, work the exercise, "Something to Do."

End this lesson with a hymn to the Blessed Sacrament.

Booklet: Appearance to the two disciples.

Part V. The Night of the Resurrection
May 2nd Week

Introduction:

Review briefly all the appearances of this first Easter Day. Let the children use the pictures to help them with the stories.

Presentation:

It was the night of the glorious Resurrection of the Savior. Not yet had Jesus appeared to His Apostles. They were in the Upper Room, behind locked doors, for they were still afraid of the Jews. But, oh, a wonderful thing happened to them. Your book tells you all about it. Let us read the story on page 168.

The teacher will read the story in a very impressive way, giving the words of the Gospel, the exact quotations, with the utmost reverence.

Now let the children study the picture and read the lesson for themselves quietly for some minutes. Then tell them:

On the night before Jesus died, He showed His special love for us by making Himself the food of our souls. This is called the Sacrament of the Holy Eucharist. On the night of His Resurrection He gave us another wonderful Sacrament. It is the Sacrament of Penance, the Sacrament of Peace.

Review again the Sacrament of Penance. Tell the story of the Prodigal Son and of the Good Thief. Dwell on the *joy* of confession, on the peace and forgiveness. Teach them the words of the priest: "I absolve thee in the Name of the Father, and of the Son, and the Holy Ghost. Amen."

End this day's lesson with another loud reading of it, and the oral answering of the questions, Answer These Questions, page 169.

End this study by having the children as a class make a special visit to Jesus in the Blessed Sacrament in thanksgiving for the Sacrament of Penance.

During the course of the day let them find the stories and read them or tell them to each other in a socialized recitation noted under Pupil's Readings.

Pupil's Readings:

Ideal Second, "He Is Risen," page 121; "Frank's Confession," page 71.

Life of Our Lord on Earth, "The Resurrection," pages 72–74.

Catholic Nursery Rhymes, "The Resurrection."

Our Sacraments, Father Kelly, "The Merciful Father," pages 26–45; "The Holy Eucharist."

Rosary Reader II, "Christ Our King," page 208.

Teacher's References:

The Holy Bible, "The Resurrection," Mark, xiv; Luke, xxiv; John, xx.

The Journeys of Jesus, Vol. III, Chapter XXI, "Morning of the Third Day"; Chapter XXXII, "Evening of the Third Day."

Jesus of Nazareth, "The Resurrection," pages 373–378; "The Risen Life," Chapter 40, pages 379–392.

The Little Ones, "Easter," page 113.

Practical Aids, "Board Drawings," pages 180–181.

Part VI. Jesus and Thomas: A Play
May 2nd Week

Introduction:

Review Questions: When did Jesus appear to the Apostles? Where were they? Why were they behind locked doors? What did Jesus say to them when He entered? What sacrament did He give us that night? Who of the Apostles do you know was not there? (Judas.) One other Apostle was missing that night. It was Thomas. Your book tells you something about Thomas and the dear Lord.

Presentation:

Let this be the usual method of reading the play. Ask the children about the time, the place, and characters required. One will read the explanatory parts, while others will read the conversational parts. After the first reading, study the picture *The Incredulity of Thomas* — Rembrandt, Guercino. Make a special study always of the picture in the text. Let the children retell the story with the help of the picture.

For a practical application of this lesson in the lives of the children, give the instruction on the attendance of services in church, of being present at family prayers, for by our absence, like Thomas, we may often lose many graces.

Remind the children to say, "My Lord and my God!" while looking at the Sacred Host at the Elevation or at Benediction of the Blessed Sacrament.

Explain the necessity of Thomas' public penance. We, too, must often make right publicly what we have done. Present little examples which occur in the life of children.

Creative Writing: Have them write a conversation between Jesus and Thomas, telling how Jesus forgives Thomas, and how sorry Thomas is.

For the final reading of the lesson, have one child step before the class and in a clear and very decided tone, like an announcer, say "Time: After the Resurrection. Place: In the Upper Room. Characters: Thomas and the other Apostles. Scene I." (Have him read all the explanatory parts of the lesson in the same way.) Let various boys of the class read the parts. Dramatize Scene I only.

End the lesson with the exercise, "Yes-and-No Test."

Part VII. Jesus in Galilee
May 3rd Week

Introduction:

Show the children the picture, *Christ's Charge to Peter*, by Raphael; *Christ Giving the Keys to St. Peter*, Reni. Tell the children the story of the picture. Have them review all the stories they remember about St. Peter. For these stories have the pictures ready which were studied during the first presentations of the same. The two stories are so closely connected that one lesson plan involves both.

Presentation:

There is another grand story about Peter and his dear Master in your books. Let us start reading it at once.

Read only to the sentence which tells how tired the Apostles were. Who remembers what happened once before when the Apostles fished all night? Let the children tell what they remember. Show the pictures of that lesson.

Now continue reading until you know what happened on this morning. Who can tell us what happened?

Read what Peter did. Why did Peter do that?

Read the part that tells you how kind Jesus was to His hungry Apostles. What did He do for them?

The next part of this story tells us of the great love of Jesus for Peter and of Peter for Jesus. Once upon a time Jesus had said to Peter: "Thou art Peter and upon this rock I will build My Church." Now the grand moment had come in the life of Peter, when Jesus would make him, Peter, the poor fisherman, head of His Church, of Jesus' only true Church, the Catholic Church.

Sister will read that part of the story and you will follow it in your book.

The teacher will read the part, Jesus and Peter, in a solemn and beautiful way.

"Now let us look at the picture once more. Can you tell me the story which the picture tells you?"

Let them repeat the story again and again. Encourage them to use the quotations as given in the lesson. Explain each quotation carefully, until every child knows what it means. Explain that the lambs in the Church are the people; the sheep are the priests and bishops; the shepherd is the Pope. Make the application personal to the children, each one of them is a little lamb of the Catholic Church. Tell them about the present pope, his name, the Vatican. Show them his picture.

"Let us read the entire lesson again." Divide the reading again into explanatory and conversational parts. Give every child a chance to do some loud reading in the lesson.

N.B.: Toward the end of the year a two weeks' project on the Catholic Church will include this lesson as well as any other points regarding the Church which ought to be learned by little children.

Kneel down, children, and tell Jesus how much you love Him. Say the prayer of St. Peter: "Lord, Thou knowest all things; Thou knowest that I love Thee."

Finish the booklet on the appearances.

Pupil's Readings:

Our Sacraments, Father Wm. Kelly; "Sacred Signs," pages 5–11; "Cleansing Water," pages 12–25; "The Merciful Father," pages 26–45.

Ideal Catholic Reader, "Frank's Confession," page 71.

Teacher's References:

The Holy Bible, Mark, xvi; Luke, xxiv; John, xx.

The Journeys of Jesus, Vol. III, Chapters 21, 22; "Evening of the Third Day," Chapter 23; "Jesus and Thomas," Chapter 24.

Jesus of Nazareth, "The Risen Life," Chapter 40, pages 379–395.

Teacher's Notes:

Review Lesson
A Radio-Program Contest

(An announcer gives the following quotations. In Part I the children will write the answers. In Part II they will give the answers orally.)

Part I
Who Said These Words:

They have taken the Lord away.

Fear not! You seek Jesus of Nazareth. He is risen. He is not here.

Mary!

Whose sins you shall forgive, they are forgiven them.

Go tell My brethren to go to Galilee. There they shall see Me.

My Lord and my God!

Cast the net on the right side of the ship.

I go afishing.

Simon, Son of John, lovest thou Me?

It is the Lord!

Peace be to you!

Rabboni!

Lord, Thou knowest all things. Thou knowest that I love Thee.

Part II
When Were These Words Said:

(The above quotations.)

Part III
Picture Contest on the Quotations

(Give the child a picture and have him tell the radio audience the story.)

Catechism Review:

1. On what day did Jesus rise from the dead?

2. How long did Jesus stay on earth after the Resurrection?

UNIT X

THE HOLIEST STORY EVER TOLD

The Ascension of the Lord
May 4th Week

Introduction:
Sing a hymn to the Savior.

Presentation:

Jesus had redeemed the world, heaven was again open to all men. He had taught His Apostles much about His Church. Peter had been made the Head of the Church. Jesus had done all the work His Father in heaven wanted Him to do on earth. He was now ready to go back to His real home, heaven. He would go to heaven to send down the Holy Ghost upon the Apostles. He was to teach them all about the Church. It was the Holy Ghost who would guide the Church to the end of the world.

Forty days had passed since Jesus rose from the dead. Something wonderful happened on this day. The story in your book, page 179, tells you about it. Let us read it.

Let them read quietly until they can tell the story. Then with the aid of the picture, *The Ascension*, Hofmann, Rembrandt, and the picture in the text, the story can be repeated as often as necessary. Study the pictures in detail.

After the picture study, turn once more to the lesson.

"Who will read the sentence that tells who were on Mount Olivet this day?

"Read the sentence that tells what Jesus wanted His Apostles to do.

"Read the part which describes how Jesus went to heaven.

"How many mind pictures can you see in the story? Which one do you like best?"

Give an instruction on heaven, the greatest joy of heaven is God. Speak of the many saints, especially of Mary, Joseph, John. Let each child tell something about any saint, his patron saint. For a description of heaven, see the Apocalypse, Chapters I, IV, XII, XIV, XXI.

Explain carefully the words of the angels: "This Jesus who is taken up from you into heaven, shall so come, as you have seen Him going into heaven." Tell them very simply of Jesus' second coming in the heavens to judge all mankind, and also each one of the children in the class.

Now let us read the entire lesson of the Ascension.

End the lesson with the exercise, "Something to Do," page 181.

Teach the second Glorious Mystery of the Rosary.

During the composition class, let them write a short composition about heaven.

Doctrine Booklet: I believe that Jesus ascended into heaven.

Teacher's References:

The Holy Bible, Matthew, xxviii; Mark, xvi; John, xxi.

The Journeys of Jesus, Vol. III, Chapter XXVI.

Teacher Tells a Story, Vol. II, "The Ascension," page 154.

Jesus of Nazareth, Chapter XLI.

Teacher's Notes:

The Birthday of the Church
May 4th Week

To the Teacher:

It is your sacred privilege and duty to instill into the hearts of youth a mighty love for the one true Church; an enthusiasm for the Faith, for religious services and practices, for the spread of the Kingdom of God on earth; to impress upon their minds a holy reverence for the Bride of Christ, and for the representatives of God on earth.

Surely we can vision a grand future as did Carl Adam in "The Spirit of Catholicism," page 208, when he says:

"And all around these outstanding saintly forms, in whom God's power and grace have won their most beautiful triumphs, shine the thousands of lesser lights, the countless little flames that have caught fire at the Heart of Jesus—from the little child that dies in the fatherly arms of God, to the old man who has scarcely escaped the danger of life, and sorrowfully prays, 'O Lord, be merciful to me a sinner.'"

O world! a sea of love and light sweeps round you.

O world, so poor and cold!

Thou art rich, thou art fair—;

O HOLY CHURCH!

Introduction:

Review Questions: How long did Jesus remain on earth after His Resurrection? What happened on the fortieth day? Why did Jesus go to heaven? Who was waiting for Him in heaven? Who is the Holy Ghost?

Presentation:

Tell the children again about the promise of Jesus to His Apostles to send the Holy Ghost. Tell how they had gone back to Jerusalem after the Ascension, back to the Upper Room to wait for the coming of the Holy Ghost. He would teach them and guide them in their work of saving souls. They had been praying nine days when the Holy Ghost came. Describe the scene very vividly.

Show the children the picture, *The Descent of the Holy Ghost,* by Fra Angelico; or *The Day of Pentecost,* by Van der Werff. After the study of these pictures, direct them to the lesson in their books on page 181.

Explain the words, *Paraclete, Pentecost.*

Let the children read the story quietly first; then ask them questions on the important sections of the lesson. Let the children formulate questions and ask them of each other.

Teach the third Glorious Mystery of the Rosary.

Give an instruction on the Holy Ghost, on sanctifying grace and grace in general received from the Holy Ghost; how all good works done for love of God give us more and more grace.

Speak to them of sanctifying grace which they received on the day of their baptism; how on that day they were made children of God and heirs of heaven. (Explain these expressions carefully.) Encourage them to be very, very careful never to lose sanctifying grace by mortal sin. If they have already done so, God will again restore it through a good Confession. To keep their soul free from sin and never to lose sanctifying grace, should be the one great aim of their life. Sanctifying grace alone gives the right to heaven.

In this instruction dwell on these questions:

Who is the Holy Ghost?

How did the Holy Ghost come down upon the Apostles?

On what day did the Holy Ghost come down upon the Apostles?

Teach the hymn, "Come, Holy Ghost." Sing it often during the work on this Unit.

Review the doctrine of the Holy Trinity. The stories of St. Patrick and St. Augustine in reference to the Trinity will help the explanation.

Review the liturgical way of making the sign of the cross.

Doctrine Booklet: I believe in the Holy Ghost.

Read the story of the Birthday of the Church aloud a few times, and close the lesson with the exercise, "Answer These Questions."

Teacher's References:

The Holy Bible, "Acts of the Apostles," Chapter II.

The Little Ones, "God of the Holy Ghost," page 69.

Teacher Tells a Story, Vol. II, "The Holy Ghost," page 162.

Teacher Tells a Story, Vol. I, "Descent of the Holy Ghost," page 107.

The Journeys of Jesus, Vol. III, "Days After the Ascension," Chapter 27.

Jesus of Nazareth, Chapter XLI.

Project:

The Catholic Church—The Kingdom of God on Earth

June 1st and 2nd Weeks

1. Tell the story of the foundation of the Church, stressing these points:

a) Review the stories of the selection and training of the Apostles. Have the children read again the lesson, "The Apostles are Chosen," page 58.

b) The promise made to Peter: Thou art Peter and upon this rock I will build My Church. Let the children retell the story with the aid of the picture.

c) Christ gives Peter the Keys. Review this story of the primacy. Let the children read the story again in their religion books on page 174, "Jesus and Peter." Have the pictures ready to help them in this review.

d) Review the story of Pentecost. Let them read the story and tell it to the class.

2. *Christ the Invisible Head of the Church.* Explain the word *invisible.* Explain the quotation: "I will be with you even to the

consummation of the world," the promise made by Jesus before His death.

Speak of the ever-presence of Jesus in the Blessed Sacrament. Reread the stories of the Last Supper.

Sing a hymn to the Blessed Sacrament.

3. *The Pope, the Visible Head of the Church.* Explain the word *visible.* Speak of the long line of popes from St. Peter to Pope Pius. Show the children a picture of Pope Pius XI. Tell them about the Great White Father in Rome, about the Vatican, about the greatest church in the world, St. Peter's in Rome. Tell them that he is also a king of a very small country. Show them pictures of anything of interest about the pope, e.g., the Swiss Guards.

Teach the song, "Long Live the Pope!" Music in *St. Gregory Hymnal,* page 122.

Talk about any other pope of great interest to the children, especially about Pope Pius X, the pope who loved children so much, the pope who gave Christ to little children in Holy Communion.

4. *Pictures.* Have the children bring pictures of different Catholic churches, making a collection of them for the classroom. Among these should be: St. Peter's in Rome, the Cathedral of their respective diocese; the home church; some of the other beautiful cathedrals and churches throughout the world, but also some of the poor missionary churches and huts. Do this to show the children that all, rich and poor alike, Jesus invites to the true Church, the Catholic Church.

Have a picture of the bishop of the diocese and one of the pastor of the respective church. Teach them the names of these people. Speak about the reverence and courtesy due to the representatives of God on earth. "If I met an angel and a priest, I would salute the priest first."—*Curé d'Ars.*

5. *Sand-Table Project.* If the table is large, arrange as many scenes as possible of Missions on it; mission of the far north, Negro missions, Indian, Japanese, Chinese. A number of small

tables can be used, each one showing one mission. On these illustrate the huts, wigwams, igloos, church, natives, priests, and Sisters. All these figures can be cut from paper and colored if desired. Dolls can be dressed, or figures can also be made from clothespins or wooden pegs. Let various groups of children work at respective missions.

Encourage the children to pray for the Missions daily; to offer their work each day for some special mission, for the missionary priests and Sisters, to say prayers for their own vocation later in life.

Form a mission society for little children or renew enthusiasm for Infant Jesus Society which is the children's missionary society in the United States.

6. *Booklets.* Pictures may be cut from magazines, *The Little Missionary,* the *Indian Sentinel,* and made into a booklet. Let the children make this as they wish. At the close of the study of the Unit, display these in the classroom.

7. *Discussions.* Suggest to the children that they, too, can be little apostles and little missionaries, by performing acts of unselfishness, gratitude, kindness, good example, prayer, mortification, and offering these for the conversion of the heathens and for sinners. Let them suggest definite situations and problems involving these and other virtues. They ought to be encouraged to give their pennies for missionary activities frequently.

8. *Posters.* Instead of a sand-table project, panel posters or the bulletin board and the burlap border can be well used to illustrate various heathen missions. Again arrange the children in groups for the work.

If they desire to make individual posters, let them do so. Offer a prize for the best poster with the best slogan. Display all these posters in the classroom and invite the other classes to see them.

9. *Dramatizations.* Divide the children into groups. Let there be a priest, a Sister, and heathen children in each group. Have Eskimo, Indian, Negro groups. Let each priest select one of the

Units in the course, and with the help of the Sister (children taking these parts) a thorough review of one Unit could be made and presented to the other groups, as though teaching it to the heathens of their group. Let the characters dress in some way suggestive of the rôle. Their religion books will serve very well for the review of the Unit.

10. *Instruction.* Give a simple instruction on what is meant by the Church, the Church on Earth, the Church in Purgatory, the Church in Heaven. Explain in the instruction what is meant by the Communion of Saints. Stress these questions of the Catechism: What is the Church? Who is the invisible Head of the Church? Who is the visible head of the Church? At this point read the lesson in the text, "The Catholic Church." The teacher will read the lesson for the class. Then the children will work the exercise at the end of the lesson.

11. *My Baptismal Promises.* Review carefully the Sacrament of Baptism. Stress these questions: What is baptism? How is baptism given? Is baptism necessary for heaven?

Arouse a great enthusiasm in the hearts of the children for their Faith from earliest childhood. Even from the first years they are entitled to the great heritage of the art, literature, culture, of their Catholic ancestry.

At this point in the project, let them turn to their reading lesson, "The Catholic Church," page 183. Have them read the lesson aloud. Then in a most solemn manner let the children sign their name to the promises at the end of the lesson, after a short explanation of each term, page 186. Children profess their Faith by showing reverence in the presence of the Blessed Sacrament, by frequent and fervent reception of the sacraments, by keeping from sin, by obeying the Commandments of God, of the Church also. Relate a few stories of how children even gave up their lives rather than their Faith. St. Pancratius.

12. *Mary, Queen of the Kingdom of God.* Sing a song to the Blessed Virgin, and tell the children about Mary, the Queen of Heaven, Queen of the Saints, Queen of the Angels, etc.

Mary, Queen of the Kingdom of God on Earth, the Catholic Church. Speak to the children of the great devotion of good Catholics to their Mother and Queen. Encourage them to say three Hail Marys daily to her for the grace of a happy death. Form a "Three Hail Mary Club," through which the children will be reminded of the prayers.

The Assumption of the Blessed Virgin Mary

Instruction:

Sing a hymn to the Blessed Virgin.

Presentation:

Study the picture, *The Assumption.* Ask the children to tell what they think the picture means. Tell them about the life of the Blessed Mother after the Ascension of Jesus. Practically all of this is traditional. Speak about St. John as her guardian, for Jesus had said to him from the cross: "Son, behold thy Mother!" Tell of her presence on Pentecost Day at the coming of the Holy Ghost; of her help to the Apostles in the infant Church; at about the age of sixty-five her death and burial; of her Assumption into heaven; the traditional story of the opening of her grave by the Apostles and the finding of the lilies instead of her body; stress the reason that her body was never to see decay—her absolute sinlessness. Explain carefully the word *Assumption.* Finally speak of the love of all good Catholics for their Mother in heaven and a true devotion to her.

"In your books is a beautiful story on the Assumption. Sister will read it for you; you follow her words in your book."

Read the story to the children very slowly and beautifully. After this first reading, explain each sentence alone.

Give an instruction stressing these ideas: Jesus wanted His dear Mother with Him in heaven. He called her soul to heaven. Mary died not through illness; she died of longing and love for her Jesus.

The Blessed Mother was so pure and holy, that she seems to have been a part of heaven given to us for a few years. Jesus wanted both the soul and the pure body of Mary with Him in heaven.

The King of heaven and all the angels and saints waited for Mary to come to her true home, heaven. She will be their queen forever and forever, queen of heaven and earth!

Teach the *Memorare* in English. Say it often with the class.

Now ask the children to tell the part of the story they like best.

End the lesson by having the children kneel and say the Hail, Holy Queen, before the statue of the Virgin Mary.

Teach the fourth and fifth Glorious Mysteries of the Rosary.

1. *Christ the King.* Study the picture in the readers, *Christ the King.* Explain the Biblical quotations of Part V, and close the lesson with the entire class giving aloud one reading of the lesson, Christ, the King of Heaven and Earth. Sing a hymn to Christ.

2. End the project by taking the children to church and there before the Blessed Sacrament, make a public thanksgiving for the Catholic Faith, by saying the Acts of Faith, Hope, Charity, very devoutly and reciting aloud the Apostles' Creed.

Teacher's References:

Practical Aids, "The Child Apostolate," pages 144–153.

BIBLIOGRAPHY

Ambrose, Sister M., O.P., *A Child's True Story* (Chicago: Lawdale Publishing House, 1928).

Aurelia, Sister Mary, O.S.F., *Practical Aids for Catholic Teachers* (Chicago: Benziger Bros., 1928).

Bible, Douay.

Brownson, Josephine Van Dyke, *To the Heart of the Child* (New York: The Encyclopedia Press, 1918).

Dennerle, Reverend George, *Leading the Little Ones to Christ* (Milwaukee: The Bruce Publishing Co., 1932).

Donoghue, Thomas, S.J., *The First Christmas* (St. Paul, Minn.; E. M. Lohmann Co.).

Dunney, Reverend Joseph, *The Mass* (New York: Macmillan Co., 1925).

Ehrman, Mary B., *The Child's Song Treasury* (Cincinnati, Ohio: Willis Music Co.).

Eaton, Mary, *The Little Ones* (St. Louis: B. Herder Co., 1925).

Eugene, Brother, O.S.F., *A Book of Religion for Elementary Schools* (New York: D. J. Sadlier).

Gasparri, Peter Cardinal, *The Catholic Catechism* (New York: Kenedy and Sons, 1932).

Gertrude, Sister M., *Catholic Nursery Rhymes* (Chicago: Benziger Bros., 1926).

Hannon, D.D., Rev. Jerome, *Teacher Tells a Story*, Books I and II (Chicago: Benziger Bros., 1925).

Herbst, Rev., *Tell Us Another* (St. Nazianz, Wisconsin: Salvatorian Fathers, 1925).

Kelly, Rev. Wm., *The Mass for Children* (St. Paul: E. M. Lohmann Co.).

———*Our First Communion* (St. Paul: E. M. Lohmann Co.).

———*Our Sacraments* (St. Paul: E. M. Lohmann Co.).

Keon, Grace, *The Life on Earth of Our Blessed Lord for Little Catholic Children* (New York: P. J. Kenedy & Sons, 1917).

139

Loyola, Mother, *First Confession* (Chicago: Benziger Bros., 1906).

————*First Communion* (Chicago: Benziger Bros., 1906).

————*The Children's Charter* (Chicago: Benziger Bros., 1911).

Matimore, Rev. P. H., *Heroes of God's Church* (New York: Macmillan Co., 1930).

————*A Child's Garden of Religion Stories* (New York: Macmillan Co., 1929).

McMunigle, M. Gertrude, *Art Education Through Religion* (Chicago: Mentzer Bush & Co.).

Mueller, Rev. F. J., *Christ's Twelve* (Milwaukee: The Bruce Publishing Co., 1931).

Religious of the Cenacle, *A Thought A Day For Lent* (New York: Paulist Press, 1931).

————*Stations of the Cross for Children* (New York: Paulist Press).

Sisters of Charity of the Blessed Virgin, *The Child's Book of Hymns* (Dubuque, Iowa: 1927).

Sisters of St. Dominic, *My Gift to Jesus* (Chicago: Lawdale Publishing House, 1929).

School Sisters of Notre Dame, *Teaching the Ten Commandments* (Milwaukee: The Bruce Publishing Co., 1931).

Sisters of Notre Dame, *Communion Verses for Little Children* (Chicago: Benziger Bros., 1912).

Sisters, Servants of the Immaculate Heart of Mary, *My Mass Book* (Chicago: Macmillan Co., 1929).

Spirago, Rev. Francis, *The Catechism Explained* (Chicago: Benziger Bros., 1899).

Stanislaus, Sister James, S.S.J., *The Journeys of Jesus* (Boston: Ginn and Co., 1927).

Thayer, Marion Dixon, *The Child On His Knees* (New York: Macmillan Co., 1928).

————*The Stations of the Cross for Children* (New York: Macmillan Co.).

————*Songs Before the Blessed Sacrament* (New York: Macmillan Co., 1932).

RESOURCE LIST

We have collected on the following pages a comprehensive list of all the recommended resources found in this manual. Based on their content and/or their frequent use in this series (often across more than one grade level) we have indicated the most essential of these with an asterisk (*), while resources which may be found on the internet are marked with a cross (†).

Second Grade Teacher Resources

*†*The Holy Bible.*

***Art Education through Religion*, Mary G. McMunigle (New York: Mentzer, Bush & Company, 1931).

†*The Catechism in Examples (5 volumes)*, Rev. D. Chisolm (London: R & T Washbourne, 1919).

†*The Catholic Education Series, Religion Book 3*, Thomas Edward Shields, M.A., Ph.D., LL.D. (Washington D.C.: The Catholic Education Press, 1915).

***Christ's Twelve*, Rev. F. J. Mueller (Milwaukee: Bruce Publishing Company, 1931).

***A Child's Garden of Religion Stories*, Rev. P. Henry Matimore, S.T.D. (New York: The Macmillan Company, 1929).

***Wonder Stories of God's People*, Rev. P. Henry Matimore, S.T.D. (New York: The Macmillan Company, 1929).

**First Communion, Mother Mary Loyola (London: Burns & Oates, 1896).

***Jesus of Nazareth: The Story of His Life Written for Children*, Mother Mary Loyola (New York: Benziger Brothers, 1906).

*The Journeys of Jesus, (3 Volumes), Sister James Stanislaus (Boston: Ginn and Company, 1927-28).

†Lent for Children: A Thought a Day, A Religious of the Cenacle (New York: The Paulist Press, 1931).

†The Life of Our Lord Written for Little Ones, Mother Mary Salome (London: Burns And Oates, 1900).

*The Little Ones: A Course of Relgious Instruction for children up to eight years, Mary Eaton (London: Sands & Co., 1925).

*Practical Aids for Catholic Teachers, Sr. Mary Aurelia, O.S.F., M.A. and Rev. Felix M. Kirsch, O.M.Cap., Litt.D. (New York: Benziger Brothers, 1928).

The Public Life of Our Lord Jesus Christ, (2 Volumes), Bishop Alban Goodier, S.J. (London: Burns, Oates & Washbourne, 1930).

The Spiritual Way, Books 1-3, Mother Margaret Bolton (Yonkers-on-Hudson: World Book Company, 1929-1930).

*Teacher Tells a Story (2 volumes), Rev. Jerome D. Hannan, D.D. (New York: Benziger Brothers, 1925).

†Teacher's Handbook to the Catechism (3 Volumes), Rev. A. Urban (New York: Joseph F. Wagner, 1902).

*Teaching the Ten Commandments, S. Mary Agnesine, S. Mary Catherine, SSND (Milwaukee: Bruce Publishing Company, 1931).

* †To the Heart of the Child, Josephine Van Dyke Brownson (New York: The Universal Knowledge Foundation, 1918).

†The Visible Church, Rt. Rev. John F. Sullivan (New York: P.J. Kenedy & Sons, 1920). (This is a rearrangement of the material found in the author's previous book, Externals of the Catholic Church.)

Second Grade Student Readers

(This list is provided for reference purposes; the majority of recommended readings from these books has been included in a newly published anthology reader to accompany this series.)

The American Cardinal Reader, Book Two, Edith M. McLaughlin (New York: Benziger Brothers, 1929).

The American Second Reader for Catholic Schools, The School Sisters of Notre Dame (Boston: D.C. Heath and Company, 1928).

Cathedral Basic Readers, Book Two, Rev. John A. O'Brien, Ph.D. (Chicago: Scott, Foresman and Company, 1931).

The Catholic Child Second Reader, Rena A. Weider, B.S. and Msgr. Charles F. McEvoy, A.M., LL.D. (Chicago: The John C. Winston Company, 1929).

The Ideal Catholic Reader, Second Reader, A Sister of St. Joseph (New York: The MacMillan Company, 1915).

Misericordia Readers Second Reader, The Sisters of Mercy (Chicago: Rand McNally & Company, 1927).

The Marquette Readers Second Reader, The Sisters of Mercy of St. Xavier (New York: The MacMillan Company, 1926).

The Marywood Readers: Happy Times (Second Reader), Sister Mary Estelle (New York: The MacMillan Company, 1930).

The Rosary Readers Second Reader, Sister Mary Henry, O.S.D. (Boston: Ginn and Company, 1927).

Additional Student Reading for Second Grade

*Catholic Nursery Rhymes, Sister Mary Gertrude, M.A. (New York: Benziger Brothers, 1925).

A Child's Way of the Cross, Mary Dixon Thayer (New York: The MacMillan Company, 1926).

Every Child's Garden (Scranton: The New Hope, 1926).

**The Life on Earth of Our Blessed Lord,* Grace Keon (St. Louis: B. Herder, 1913).

My Gift to Jesus, Sisters of the Order of St. Dominic (Chicago: Lawndale Publishing Company, 1929).

My Mass Book, Sisters Servants of the IHM (New York: The MacMillan Company, 1929).

**Our Sacraments,* Rev. William R. Kelly (New York: Benziger Brothers, 1927).

†*Stations of the Cross for Children,* A Religious of the Cenacle (New York: The Paulist Press, 1936).

THE HIGHWAY TO HEAVEN SERIES

Prepared in the Catechetical Institute of Marquette University
(In co-operation with a group of Priests and Sisters teaching in the elementary schools)

GRADE	TEXT	MANUAL CURRICULUM IN RELIGION (1st to 8th Grade inclusive)
1	**THE BOOK OF THE HOLY CHILD** By *Sister Mary Bartholomew, O.S.F.* 96 pages	First Grade Teachers Plan Book and Manual
2	**THE LIFE OF MY SAVIOR** By a School Sister of Notre Dame 196 pages	Second Grade Teachers Plan Book and Manual
3	**THE LIFE OF THE SOUL** Prepared in the Catechetical Institute of Marquette University *Edward A. Fitzpatrick, Ph.D.* Educational Director 144 pages	Third Grade Teachers Plan Book and Manual
4	**BEFORE CHRIST CAME** By a School Sister of Notre Dame 256 pages	Fourth Grade Teachers Plan Book and Manual
5	**THE VINE AND THE BRANCHES** By the *Rev. R. G. Bandas, Ph.D.Agg., S.T.D. et M.* and a School Sister of Notre Dame 320 pages	Fifth Grade Teachers Plan Book and Manual
6	**THE SMALL MISSAL**	Workbook for the Missal
7 & 8	**THE HIGHWAY TO GOD** Prepared in the Catechetical Institute of Marquette University *Edward A. Fitzpatrick, Ph.D.* Educational Director 420 pages	Practical Problems in Religion By the *Rev. R. G. Bandas, Ph.D.Agg., S.T.D. et M.* (Answers problems in text)

www.ingramcontent.com/pod-product-compliance
Lightning Source LLC
Chambersburg PA
CBHW060826050426
42453CB00008B/604